The Way That Leads There

The Way That Leads There

AUGUSTINIAN REFLECTIONS
ON THE CHRISTIAN LIFE

Gilbert Meilaender

WILLIAM B. EERDMANS PUBLISHING COMPANY
GRAND RAPIDS, MICHIGAN / CAMBRIDGE, U.K.

Published 2006 by

Wm. B. Eerdmans Publishing Co.

255 Jefferson Ave. S.E., Grand Rapids, Michigan 49503 /

P.O. Box 163, Cambridge CB3 9PU U.K.

Printed in the United States of America

11 10 09 08 07 06   7 6 5 4 3 2 1

Library of Congress Cataloging-in-Publication Data

Meilaender, Gilbert, 1946-

The way that leads there: Augustinian reflections on the Christian life /
Gilbert Meilaender.

p.   cm.

ISBN-10: 0-8028-3213-X / ISBN-13: 978-0-8028-3213-9 (pbk.: alk. paper)

1. Augustine, Saint, Bishop of Hippo.   2. Christian life.   I. Title.

BR65.A9M45 2006

241'.042 — dc22

2006008541

www.eerdmans.com

To Jonathan, Charlotte, Miriam, and Veronika

Ibi vacabimus et videbimus,
videbimus et amabimus,
amabimus et laudabimus

CONTENTS

PREFACE

I N A N Y humanistic field of study there are thinkers to whom we regularly return — in part because the reach of their influence has shaped the field in important ways, but also because the power of their thinking continues to make them stimulating "conversation partners" for us. In this book I return to Saint Augustine, to probe, with his help, some aspects of the moral life. Of course, this is not the only way in which one might return to Augustine. We might take him as the object of purely historical study, or we might, for example, write commentary on some of his most important works. Such study has been and continues to be done, and we all profit from it.

Here, however, I take him up for the somewhat different reason that, in thinking about certain perennial problems of the moral life, I find that he seldom fails to illumine my own sight or provoke me to fresh thought. When I ask myself what it is about Augustine that makes him seem so apt a conversation partner, I usually conclude that it is his ability to "worry" about things. In *Coming Apart,* the memoir of his early years as a professor, Roger Rosenblatt suggests that the best teaching is "being overheard as one worries aloud about a subject." If that is the criterion — and I think it is — Augustine seems to me to get high marks as a teacher. In particular, it is often at those places where one is tempted to dismiss him as misguided, or even comical, that listening to Augustine worry over a subject can set us free from the limits that confine us.

I have returned to him, therefore, to think about some questions that never go away. I began with the old puzzle about the relation between desire and duty in the moral life, and I moved out from there to think about realms of life (politics and sex) in which we seek (and often fail) to bring desire and duty into harmonious order. The vision of life that emerges — at least as I read Augustine — is one whose power lies chiefly in his sense that the way that leads to God (and, hence, to fulfillment) is a way that often hurts and wounds us. His description of Roman life — even when the empire was at its grandest — as having "the fragile brilliance of glass" is in many respects his vision of life at every time and place.

Try though I have to learn from those whose scholarly lives are largely devoted to Augustine, it should be clear that I am not among their company. I make use of him in different ways and for different purposes, and in the concluding chapter I offer a brief apologia for doing so. I have used a variety of translations — usually those that for one reason or another I have read for years. In particular, I have used Henry Bettenson's (Penguin Books) translation of *The City of God* and Rex Warner's wonderfully lively (New American Library) translation of *The Confessions*. An earlier version of chapter 5 appeared in the *Journal of Religious Ethics* (Spring 2001).

ABBREVIATIONS

Aquinas

ST	*Summa theologiae*

Augustine

C. mend.	*Contra mendacium*
Conf.	*The Confessions*
Ep.	*Epistula*
Solil.	*Soliloquies*
Trin.	*On the Trinity*

DESIRE

In Westwood Cemetery in Oberlin, Ohio, in an area of the cemetery known as Missionary Rest, a marker at the gravesite of one of the children of an Oberlin missionary reads simply:

> Dear Jesus
> You know that I love you
> Take me to yourself[1]

The marker expresses with profound simplicity a certain kind of human neediness, a longing that can be satisfied only in union with God. Moreover, at least in this simple expression, that longing does not seem presumptuous, nor does it suggest that God becomes merely a means to one's own happiness. On the contrary, it is hard to read the marker as anything other than a natural and appropriate expression of the fact that love seeks union and, in particular, that human beings long to enjoy the presence of God. Nevertheless, such a needy, desirous

1. I am indebted to Fred Lassen for calling this marker to my attention.

I

love has sometimes seemed problematic in the tradition of Christian reflection on the moral life.

Consider the contrasting impulses in two passages from C. S. Lewis. Near the end of *Surprised by Joy*, having recounted his conversion as the story of one who was longing for joy, Lewis notes that there was at first no necessary connection for him between the joy he had been seeking and the God he found. "I had," he writes,

> been brought up to believe that goodness was goodness only if it were disinterested, and that any hope of reward or fear of punishment contaminated the will. If I was wrong in this (the question is really much more complicated than I then perceived) my error was most tenderly allowed for. I was afraid that threats or promises would demoralize me; no threats or promises were made. The commands were inexorable, but they were backed by no "sanctions." God was to be obeyed simply because He was God. Long since, through the gods of Asgard, and later through the notion of the Absolute, He had taught me how a thing can be revered not for what it can do to us but for what it is in itself.[2]

That is Lewis's recollection of how he felt when "in the Trinity Term of 1929 I gave in, and admitted that God was God, and knelt and prayed: perhaps, that night, the most dejected and reluctant convert in all England."[3]

By the time Lewis preached a sermon titled "The Weight of Glory" in 1942, he had begun to appreciate the complications

2. C. S. Lewis, *Surprised by Joy* (New York: Harcourt, Brace and World, 1955), p. 231.
3. Lewis, *Surprised by Joy*, pp. 228-29.

he had earlier missed. The governing virtue of Christian life, he now wants to say, is not disinterested unselfishness but, rather, love. Unselfishness as an ideal suggests primarily that we forgo our own good; love calls and moves us to serve the good of others (which we can do only if they in turn desire some good that will make them happy). "The New Testament has lots to say about self-denial, but not about self-denial as an end in itself. . . . Indeed, if we consider the unblushing promises of reward and the staggering nature of the rewards promised in the Gospels, it would seem that our Lord finds our desires, not too strong, but too weak. We are half-hearted creatures, fooling about with drink and sex and ambition when infinite joy is offered us."[4] Genuine love, it now seems to Lewis, is characterized by a childlike humility that can acknowledge its need to give and receive pleasure.

The tension between these contrasting impulses has characterized Christian thought from the start. In his classic work *The Vision of God*, Kenneth Kirk observes how there appear regularly in the Gospels two contrasting strains of thought — which he calls the mercenary and the disinterestedness strain — and how they "appear to contradict and neutralize one another."[5] With respect to the mercenary strain, in which recompense and reward are emphasized, Kirk notes that "even the most fundamental and far-reaching precepts of Christian duty are commended by the hope of recompense."[6] It would be almost impossible to improve upon the concatenation of passages that Kirk uses to illustrate his claim. Charity: "But when

4. C. S. Lewis, "The Weight of Glory," in *The Weight of Glory and Other Addresses* (Grand Rapids: Eerdmans, 1965), pp. 1-2.

5. Kenneth E. Kirk, *The Vision of God*, 2nd ed. (London: Longmans, Green, and Co., 1932), p. 142.

6. Kirk, p. 141.

you give a feast, invite the poor, the maimed, the lame, the blind, and you will be blessed, because they cannot repay you. You will be repaid at the resurrection of the just" (Luke 14:13-14). Humility: "I tell you, this man [the tax collector] went down to his house justified rather than the other; for everyone who exalts himself will be humbled, but he who humbles himself will be exalted" (Luke 18:14). Watchfulness and prayer: "Blessed is that servant whom his master when he comes will find so doing. Truly, I say to you, he will set him over all his possessions" (Luke 12:43-44). Loving enemies: "But love your enemies, and do good, and lend, expecting nothing in return; and your reward will be great, and you will be sons of the Most High" (Luke 6:35). Forgiveness: "For if you forgive men their trespasses, your heavenly Father also will forgive you" (Matt. 6:14). Secret piety: "But when you give alms, do not let your left hand know what your right hand is doing, so that your alms may be in secret; and your Father who sees in secret will reward you" (Matt. 6:3-4).

At the same time, however, the mere presence of the book of Job in the Bible is sufficient to remind us that God does not exist merely to make us happy — that he is to be honored simply because he is God, and not only because of what he can do to fulfill our desires. We're told that God "answered" Job out of the whirlwind (38:1), but the answer is more like a bludgeoning. Most telling is the fact that God's "answer" often takes no direct account of Job's — or humankind's — concern. God "bring[s] rain on a land where no man is" (38:26). Utterly oblivious to the dependence of human beings on rainfall, God pours rain on the land where no one is — not to make us happy, perhaps even to offend our expectation that God should exist primarily to serve us, certainly as an indication that God must be revered for reasons that go well beyond his care for humanity. Luther makes a similar point in his commentary on the Magnificat. Mary, he writes, shows us how properly to magnify God — namely, "to count only Him great and lay claim to nothing."[7] This emphasis, quite common in Luther's writing, has its biblical ground in the character of the God whom Job encounters. Thus, Luther can also say of Mary that "she sets things in their proper order when she calls God her Lord before calling Him her Savior. . . . Thereby she teaches us to love and praise God for Himself alone, and in the right order, and not selfishly to seek anything at His hands."[8] The last words of this sentence — which may begin to suggest that seeking anything from God is selfish, as if the marker on that child's grave might be misguided — should remind us of the danger to which such an emphasis can easily fall prey, a danger to which Luther was not immune, as we will note later.

Saint Augustine's *Confessions* provides a rich text for reflecting upon these contrasting impulses of Christian life — a desire for union with God, together with a sense that God does not exist simply to make us happy. Indeed, Augustine has in considerable measure set the terms in which Christians have thought about this tension. From the *Confessions*, a book filled with memorable lines, few passages have been more often cited than the programmatic statement at the very outset: "[Y]ou have made us for yourself, and our hearts are restless until they can find rest in you" (I.I). What is perhaps only implied in I.I, Augustine says explicitly elsewhere in the *Confessions:* "And this is the happy life — to rejoice in you and to you and because of you. This is the happy life; there is no other"

7. Martin Luther, *The Magnificat,* in *Luther's Works,* vol. 21 (St. Louis: Concordia, 1956), p. 308.
8. Luther, *The Magnificat,* p. 309.

(10.22). No happiness, no fulfillment or flourishing, is available unless the heart rests in God.

How, a believer might wonder, could it be otherwise? Yet, some have thought it deeply troubling and finally mistaken, even if profoundly so. Augustine's theme of the "restless heart" seems to place him squarely within the classical tradition of eudaimonism. Thus, Aristotle says in the *Nicomachean Ethics* (1.4) that all people desire happiness *(eudaimonia)*, even though they often disagree about where such happiness may be found. Augustine likewise puzzles at length (*Conf.* 10.21-23) over how it can be that all want to be happy, and that to rest in God constitutes the happy life — but that nonetheless not all look to God for the happiness they desire.

Should we be troubled by Augustine's belief that we are characterized by a longing for God — that, in particular, we desire God for the sake of our own happiness? There are at least three important — and different — sorts of reasons why we might be troubled. First, the seeming "anthropocentrism" of the eudaimonistic quest — which, grasping only one of those two contrasting impulses, threatens to lose the tension between them — may appear selfish. "[W]hen I seek you, my God, I am seeking the happy life," Augustine says (10.20). God seems to be important primarily as One who satisfies a human longing, One who makes us happy — and this, inevitably, sounds selfish.[9] In order to guard against just such a conclusion, in order to assert that our longing for God is not simply a desire for our own benefit, Saint Thomas Aquinas (centuries later) distinguished *amor amicitiae* from *amor concupiscentiae.*

9. Exactly the conclusion famously drawn by Anders Nygren. "Even though [for Augustine] God is described as the highest good, this does not alter the fact that He is degraded to the level of a means for the satisfaction of human desire." *Agape and Eros* (London: SPCK, 1953), p. 500.

The first love "has the character of friendship" in that "we love someone so as to wish good to him." If, by contrast, we love someone not because we wish him well but because we gain something from him, that is "love not of friendship, but of a kind of concupiscence" (*ST* IIaIIae, q. 23, a. 1). And, according to Aquinas, charity for God is a love of friendship — a benevolent, not a concupiscent, love.

In attempting to solve one difficulty, Aquinas may create others. The language of friendship implies a kind of equality and reciprocity in love that seems ill suited to describe our relation to God, who always has the initiative in that relation; moreover, such language may seem to lose a sense of our neediness and dependence on God. But it does at least give Saint Thomas a way to make clear that our love for God is not simply a self-serving desire for our own benefit. Explaining why charity is the greatest of the virtues, more excellent even than faith or hope, he tries to make this explicit: "[F]aith and hope attain God indeed in so far as we derive from Him the knowledge of truth or the acquisition of good, whereas charity attains God Himself that it may rest in Him, but not that something may accrue to us from Him" (IIaIIae, q. 23, a. 6). Thus, when we think with Augustine about our desire to find happiness in God, we are thinking about an issue that had been important before he wrote the *Confessions* and that by no means disappeared in succeeding centuries — the danger of an anthropocentrism for which God is important primarily as one who makes us happy.

A second puzzling and perhaps troubling feature of Augustine's depiction of the restless heart is buried in the suggestion that everyone desires God. "[T]he happy life is joy in truth, which means joy in you, who are truth, God. . . . This is the happy life, which all desire; this life which alone is happy all desire; joy in truth is what all desire" (*Conf.* 10.23). We can express this problem almost as the inversion of our first worry. "To seek God is to seek the happy life" — that appeared selfish. "To seek the happy life is to seek God" — that, together with the premise that all seek the happy life, suggests that there is no one who does not long to rest in God. All are engaged in fundamentally the same religious quest, whether they know it or not. This is not unlike the sentiment expressed by Vergil in almost the last words he speaks to Dante in the *Divine Comedy*. Having guided Dante through purgatory to the very brink of the earthly paradise, Vergil says (in canto XXVII of the *Purgatorio*):

> This is the day your hungry soul shall be
> fed on the golden apples men have sought
> on many different boughs so ardently.

The religious quest is characterized, finally, not by its object (the true God), but by a kind of longing or desire integral to our humanity. From this different angle also, therefore, Augustine's eudaimonistic quest seems inherently anthropocentric.

A third feature of the restless heart theme has also seemed problematic. Of the truths learned by the philosophers, Augustine writes, "But, Lord God of truth, does a man please you by knowing all these things? For the man who knows them all, but does not know you, is unhappy, and happy is the man who knows you, even if he does not know these other things. And he who knows both you and them is not the happier because of them but is only happy because of you" (*Conf.* 5.4). To take God seriously as the object of our heart's desire seems, inevitably, to suggest that all other objects of love are "[t]oys and trifles, utter vanities," as Augustine describes the "mistresses" that pulled at him as the crisis of his life came to a head (8.11). "Are you getting rid of us?" they ask (8.11). And the answer seems to be yes. "For you converted me to you in such a way that I no longer sought a wife nor any other worldly hope" (8.12). And why not? "Smoke has no weight," as Augustine puts it in the *City of God* (5.17).

There is something deeply biblical about this sense that God's claim upon the human heart must be whole and entire. After all, "the kingdom of heaven is like treasure hidden in a field, which a man found and covered up; then in his joy he goes and sells all that he has and buys that field" (Matt. 13:44). More hauntingly still, Jesus says that "if anyone comes to me and does not hate his own father and mother and wife and children and brothers and sisters, yes, and even his own life, he cannot be my disciple" (Luke 14:26). If no object of love other than God can really satisfy the restless heart's desire, then it is hard to know why the heart that has found God should need or love any other object. In the end, the anthropocentric quest for *eudaimonia* may seem to turn back upon itself and devour itself, with the seeming disappearance of human beings as objects of love. And yet, the same scriptures that articulate the need to love God without any rival teach us that we are bound by two love commands — to love God with all one's heart and, somehow, to have heart left to love the neighbor (Mark 12:30-31).

On the face of it, then, our desire for God seems selfish, seems to end in an amorphous God whom all love in their different ways, and seems to leave place for only one object of our love. To think again with Augustine about the restless heart is to return to some perennial problems for Christian life.

To Seek God Is to Seek the Happy Life:
A Selfish Quest?

Augustine sounds the theme of the restless heart in the opening paragraph of the *Confessions,* and it is instructive to note how he does this:

> *Great art thou, O Lord, and greatly to be praised; great is thy power, and thy wisdom is infinite.* And man wants to praise you, man who is only a small portion of what you have created and who goes about carrying with him his own mortality, the evidence of his own sin and evidence that *Thou resistest the proud.* Yet still man, this small portion of creation, wants to praise you. You stimulate him to take pleasure in praising you, because you have made us for yourself, and our hearts are restless until they can find rest in you. . . . [A]nd they that find Him shall praise Him. (1.1)

It seems right that we should desire to be in the presence of the God who made us, but the desire Augustine here articulates cannot be described as a merely selfish desire to possess God. His desire is not to possess but to praise — or, perhaps, in praising to possess. Thus, for example, John Burnaby notes that for Augustine love can persist in heaven even when the desire to possess has been satisfied. Desire gives way to delight because the "need has been met by the good appropriate to it."[10] Moreover, as only a "small portion of creation," we would deceive ourselves to suppose that the Creator exists simply to make us happy. The truth, as Aquinas notes in explaining why

---

10. John Burnaby, *Amor Dei: A Study of the Religion of St. Augustine* (London: Hodder and Stoughton, 1938), p. 96.

our love for God is not simply acquisitive longing, is that "the Divine good is greater in itself than our share of good in enjoying Him" (*ST* IIaIIae, q. 26, a. 3, ad. 3). Only a few sentences from the end of the *Confessions,* Augustine makes a similar point: "[Y]ou, the Good, which is in need of no other good, are always at rest, because you are your own rest" (13.37). In such a God the restless human heart will find peace "in the Sabbath of eternal life" (13.36).

We will therefore surely misread the *Confessions* if we overlook the way Augustine frames his story, the human story. It is less a story of our need to possess than to praise God. But it is a story of need. We are so made that we must look to God for our happiness. This "small portion of creation" that is humanity cannot claim to be self-sufficient and can find no happiness apart from God. That we turn to God most readily and most often when our need is great no doubt indicates that our love is not yet perfected, but it is surely better to call to God from our neediness than (proudly?) to refuse to acknowledge creaturely need.

In seeking God one seeks the happy life. This can of course be a strategy or a technique of manipulation. "For," as Augustine writes to a correspondent, "the man who only fears the flames of hell is afraid not of sinning, but of being burned" (*Ep.* 145.4). But Augustine does not seek God in order that he may thereby live a happy life; he seeks God in order to delight in his presence.[11] The union he desires is more than agreement in will. However important that may be, however much lovers who are separated may take comfort in knowing that they are of one mind, they still want presence

---

11. Thus Burnaby, p. 109: "To 'enjoy' is to cleave to something in the love which is enjoyment, not by means of the love which is desire."

— personal contact. Such union — of praise and presence — is always a source of joy, but it is the presence itself that is, for human beings, fulfillment. It would be possible, I suppose, to want the joy that comes from being in God's presence without the presence itself, just as it would be possible to want the pleasure that comes from marriage without the presence of the beloved (if the pleasure could be provided, say, by manipulation of the brain). But this would be a degradation rather than a fulfillment of our humanity. Similarly with Augustine's desire to find happiness in God. The point is not to have joy but to rest in God's presence, which will of course bring joy to one who loves God. We must imagine lovers who want to be with each other. Naturally, they know that being together will make them happy, but it would miss the point to suppose that they wanted simply the happiness — and not the presence of the loved one. Likewise, delighting in the presence and praise of God just is, for human beings, fulfillment. It is the free relinquishing of our plans and projects in order to receive what cannot be planned, intended, or manipulated: loving union with God. And it requires a kind of forgetfulness of self — or, perhaps better, a self that is constituted not in isolation but in the giving and receiving that is the bond of love. Without that self-forgetfulness no self-fulfillment is possible.

Looking to God for our happiness is therefore the worship creatures offer their Creator, and it requires a measure of self-forgetfulness. We can call this a loss of self (in the praise of God) or an expansion of self (as one flourishes in God). It makes little difference which way we describe it, so long as we understand how closely the two are related. In explaining how a literary work may provide "an enlargement of our being," C. S. Lewis described the experience well:

Good reading, therefore, though it is not essentially an affectional or moral or intellectual activity, has something in common with all three. In love we escape from our self into one other. In the moral sphere, every act of justice or charity involves putting ourselves in the other person's place and thus transcending our own competitive particularity. In coming to understand anything we are rejecting the facts as they are for us in favour of the facts as they are. . . . In love, in virtue, in the pursuit of knowledge, and in the reception of the arts, we are doing this. Obviously this process can be described either as an enlargement or as a temporary annihilation of the self. But that is an old paradox; "he that loseth his life shall save it."[12]

"In love we escape from our self into one other." And in love of God we escape from our self into that One Other who is not a private good, but a common good, "the good of all things" (*Conf.* 3.8).

Thus, while Augustine can unself-consciously pray to "embrace my one and only good, which is you," he can also immediately add: "And not to love you, is not this in itself misery enough?" (1.5). Failing to rest in the God whom we are made to praise is missing the very meaning of our created being — misery enough, indeed. Thus, to seek God is indeed to seek the happy life, to seek to flourish as a human being. So far is this longing from being self-centered that we might almost say the opposite is the case. Not to desire God, to seek the self-sufficiency of an "unreal liberty" (3.8) that denies one's need for God, is to place one's own self at the very center of things.

12. C. S. Lewis, *An Experiment in Criticism* (Cambridge: University Press, 1969), p. 138.

Doing so risks "the loss of everything by setting our love more upon our own private good than upon you, the good of all things" (3.8). God calls us out of ourselves — and in answering that call we become more fully ourselves.

How complicated this actually is may be seen if we briefly consider the diametrically opposed standpoints developed in Anders Nygren's *Agape and Eros* and Servais Pinckaers's *The Sources of Christian Ethics*. As is well known, Nygren regards Augustine's eudaimonism as "egocentric" in relation to God. That is, "the religious relationship is dominated essentially by man."[13] Even though, of course, Augustine regards God as the highest possible object of our love, "this does not alter the fact that He is degraded to the level of a means for the satisfaction of human desire" (p. 500). In a truly theocentric view, by contrast, God must be at the center. "Any thought of man's raising himself up to the Divine life is felt to be sheer titanic pride" (p. 206).

Pinckaers grounds his discussion of eudaimonism in the distinction between freedom of indifference and freedom for excellence. If we picture human freedom as "freedom of indifference," we begin with a bare will, a simple power of choosing. A person, then, is not someone who longs for a particular fulfillment, who is drawn toward any particular good; rather, a person is simply one who is free to choose between contraries. And the point of morality is not to direct us toward our happiness but to show us how to choose rightly — by, for example, choosing in accord with God's commands. By contrast, the "freedom for excellence" model makes the *rational* will, not simply the power to choose, central to our picture of a human

---

13. Nygren, p. 205. Parenthetical page numbers in the remainder of this paragraph refer to this work.

person — and in so doing opens up space for eudaimonism. In the very structure of creation, that rational will naturally inclines to seek the good and to know the truth. A human being "can never renounce this natural order of things, nor be prevented from desiring it."[14] From this perspective the point of morality is to help perfect us as the persons we naturally desire to be, a longing for fulfillment that we should never renounce. When we pursue our happiness, therefore, Pinckaers would say we are seeking to become what God has made us to be. This is not a selfish quest; instead, it is an honest acknowledgment that we are not self-creators who can forge their own happiness.

According to Pinckaers, the freedom of indifference that — in order to rule out any anthropocentric use of God as a means to our satisfaction — renounces even the desire for our own happiness, conceals "a primitive passion" that is "the human will to self-affirmation."[15] That would be his verdict on Nygren's man of faith who uproots the eudaimonistic longing in order to let God be God. According to Nygren, the acquisitive longing for God that puts our desire to rest in God at the center of the religious life conceals "sheer titanic pride."[16] That would be his verdict on Pinckaers's depiction of freedom for excellence.

What Nygren calls theocentric, Pinckaers understands as anthropocentric. What Nygren calls egocentric, Pinckaers describes as a humble realization that only God can constitute our happiness, that we are not self-creators. Each would detect sinful pride buried at the heart of the other's system. For Pinckaers the redemptive work of God in Jesus is essentially

14. Servais Pinckaers, *The Sources of Christian Ethics* (Washington, D.C.: Catholic University of America Press, 1995), pp. 332f.

15. Pinckaers, p. 338.

16. Nygren, p. 206.

continuous with the deepest desire of human life, and only as God draws our life into his own incarnate being can human desire reach the fruition for which it has been created. For Nygren any tendency to suppose that God must somehow satisfy a desire that comes naturally to our hearts must be put to death and buried with Christ — so that, in the great *discontinuity* of resurrection, a new self that asks nothing of God and receives everything from God may come forth.

Perhaps the truth is more complex than either author allows (since, after all, in the Christian story incarnation is directed toward cross and resurrection, and since the risen Christ, however altered his state, is the same Jesus who was buried). Pinckaers cannot be right to suppose that a freedom of indifference, and its accompanying morality centered on obligation, must necessarily express a human self-affirmation that grounds morality not in God but in bare human will and choice; for, after all, as Pinckaers well knows, one can look to God's commands for the key to the moral life. In so doing, in bending the knee and acknowledging that the Author of our being has authority over us, we would hardly be placing human will at the center of the moral life. Nygren cannot be right to suppose that Augustine's eudaimonism, with its depiction of a love whose nature it is to desire God, must simply be a refined form of selfishness; for, after all, as Nygren himself grants, for Augustine this is simply a way of saying "that we, unlike God, have not life in ourselves and of ourselves, but from Him. *Desire is the mark of the creature.*"[17]

Pinckaers is right to see that we should never construct an

---

17. Nygren, p. 479. For the possibility of a "nonpossessive eros," see William Werpehowski, "Anders Nygren's *Agape and Eros*," in *The Oxford Handbook of Theological Ethics*, ed. Gilbert Meilaender and William Werpehowski (Oxford: Oxford University Press, 2005), pp. 442-45.

ethic that requires us to deny our creaturely need for God. When and where Nygren fails to see that, he invariably goes wrong, and anyone drawn to Nygren's characterization of agape will need to guard against such a defective vision of our created nature. Nygren, however, is right to see that a eudaimonistic ethic can all too easily picture the Christian life as largely continuous with our natural inclinations — as if sacrifice were not integral to that life. When, referring to Ephesians 4:13, Pinckaers describes Christ as the perfect, fully mature human being,[18] we must recall where that perfect man ended in human history — namely, on a cross. That should make us a little wary of the sort of description Pinckaers gives of one who is morally mature, in whom the freedom for excellence is well developed: "Our freedom reaches maturity precisely with our capacity to balance the twofold dimension of personality and openness to others, interiority and outreach, living 'for self' and 'for others.'"[19] One may legitimately wonder whether this depiction of "balance" in the moral life adequately captures the sheer immoderate self-forgetfulness that characterizes a bond of love. Because the Creator calls us out of ourselves to himself, looking to God for our happiness is inevitably marked by self-forgetfulness, and anyone drawn to Pinckaers's eudaimonism will need to acknowledge that there can be no other road to happiness. That truth is written into our created being.

Moreover, as Nygren rightly emphasizes, there is a second reason — grounded not in our creatureliness but in our sin — why the quest for happiness must be self-forgetful. Augustine emphasizes at the outset, we recall, that "this small portion of

18. Pinckaers, p. 368.
19. Pinckaers, p. 367.

creation" that is humanity does not want to be needy or dependent. We can flourish only when we praise God; yet, we do not want to offer the praise that in its very nature suggests that our happiness must be God's gift. And so we are trapped by the division within our nature — as fundamentally needy beings who nonetheless desire self-sufficiency. Here and now, in this life, placing our happiness in God will require that we relinquish the desire for happiness on our own terms and cultivate instead the patience to wait for God. The way to fulfillment of self may therefore seem more like sacrifice of self. Augustine does not suppose that, along the way, we will necessarily feel that our heart's longing has been satisfied. God wills to draw us out of ourselves, wills that we should praise him. But inexplicably — as inexplicable as the theft of pears Augustine recounts in book 2 — our desire to lose ourselves in the praise of God is regularly challenged by our desire to have other good things not simply as God's gift but as our own achievement and possession.

By the time we come to book 8 of Augustine's story, his intellectual difficulties have been resolved. He has shucked off the teaching of the Manichees, solved (with the aid of the Platonists) his difficulties in comprehending the nature of a spiritual being, and discovered (what the Platonists did not know) the wonder of Christ's incarnation in which God takes the initiative to answer human need. His problem now is not intellectual but volitional. "I no longer desired to be more certain of you, only to stand more firmly in you." He is, in effect, still placing himself at the center of things. "I had now found that pearl of great price, and I ought to have sold all that I had and bought it. But I hesitated" (8.1). He has been asserting himself when he in fact needs to be "stripped naked" (8.7) and set free from himself. And the great "conversion" experience in the garden does just that: it frees him not from the longing for God but from the sinful illusion that he could forge his own felicity. He quickly discovers, however, that life-transforming as this experience has been, it has done no more than set him on the way toward fulfillment. Along that way a good bit of sacrifice will be called for.

Because our desires remain disordered even after the fundamental division within the self has been overcome, the God who is our happiness may not make us happy here and now. "He serves you best who is not so anxious to hear from you what he wills as to will what he hears from you" (10.26). In this "far country," where Augustine says he wasted his substance "upon false and prostitute desires" (4.16), the path to self-fulfillment must often seem more like self-sacrifice. We can look for happiness to the good things that draw us here and now, even though they will not finally satisfy the heart's longing. Or we can redirect that longing to the God who can satisfy it but in whom we cannot rest here and now. That is, we can have a sham happiness that will not really satisfy — or we can relinquish the desire to grasp the happy life here and now, leaving open in our being a gaping wound that God must fill in his own good time. "Here I have the power but not the wish to stay; there I wish to be but cannot; both ways, miserable" (10.40).

We should be reluctant to adopt strategies that invite us to underplay the importance of self-sacrifice in the Christian life, as John Milbank, for example, does in an essay entitled "The Ethics of Self-Sacrifice." To avoid obliterating the presence of others in the mutuality of love, he almost portrays self-sacrificial love as obliteration of oneself. Indeed, he goes so far as to argue that the notion of a unilateral gift is "barely coherent." Even our awareness that we are giving a gift "cancel[s] the gratuity of the gift," he suggests. Hence, a truly unilateral gift "would have to be to an absolutely anonymous other."[20] This is rather like Kierkegaard exalting works of love for the dead as the proof of love's genuineness. The point of self-sacrificial love is not (as Kierkegaard sometimes seemed to think) to persuade ourselves that we are being sacrificial; on the contrary, the focus of attention is the loved one. Moreover, it is precisely such attention to the needs of others, rather than simply a concern to be a person of a certain sort, that may sometimes elicit from us a love that seeks nothing in return. (Milbank's language is systematically ambiguous. He sometimes writes of a gift that "expects" nothing in return or of giving without "guarantee" of return, or of being "indifferent" to return. These are not interchangeable, and none of them seems adequate to the character of Christian self-sacrificing love. The best formulation is one Milbank uses least: that the lover should "hope" for a return — which hope need not, of course, turn one's act into a form of self-seeking.) One who gives self-sacrificially may experience pleasure at thus serving another, but that hardly makes it right for Milbank to suggest that such an act is really a form of self-love. Were that the case, we would be entirely unable to distinguish an act that gave me pleasure because it was clearly to my advantage from an act that gave me pleasure because (even at some cost to myself) it clearly served the need of a friend. Thus, as Jean Bethke Elshtain puts it, "the Christian is not afraid that he or she will lose something by offering him or herself. That is what the ethic of *caritas* is about — not moralistic self-abnegation but an abundant overflowing of the fullness of life."[21]

20. John Milbank, "The Ethics of Self-Sacrifice," *First Things*, no. 91 (March 1999): 33-38, here 36.
21. Jean Bethke Elshtain, *Augustine and the Limits of Politics* (Notre Dame, Ind.: University of Notre Dame Press, 1995), p. 36.

God will make happy those who rest in him, but as Lewis writes in *The Four Loves*, "there is no good applying to Heaven for earthly comfort. Heaven can give heavenly comfort; no other kind."[22] Hence, the grace that makes us happy may hurt here and now. From our selfish neediness, our desire for a God who is simply the means to our own happiness, God's grace slowly creates "a full, childlike and delighted acceptance of our Need, a joy in total dependence."[23] Whether we can attain such purity of heart in this life is uncertain, but when — and whenever — such a love has been worked in the human heart, anthropocentrism will have been overthrown as, simultaneously, the *anthropos* is fulfilled.

Thus, because we are needy creatures and sinful creatures, forgetfulness and even sacrifice of self must often characterize the journey to rest in God, the journey that will bring us to our happiness. Nevertheless, necessary as it is to acknowledge the seeming loss of self experienced along the way, we should not speak of the way (self-sacrifice) as if it were the goal (joy in God's presence). If we fear too greatly the "mercenary" strain in the Gospels with its promise of reward, even our attempts to exalt God may lose what Lewis calls "a full, childlike and delighted acceptance of our Need." For example, commenting on Romans 9:3 (where Saint Paul says he would pray that he himself be "cut off from Christ" if thereby his Jewish kinsmen might turn to Christ and be saved),[24] Luther writes that Paul's words will seem

22. C. S. Lewis, *The Four Loves* (New York: Harcourt Brace Jovanovich, 1960), p. 190.

23. Lewis, *The Four Loves*, p. 180.

24. I would follow Cranfield in taking this construction to be a prayer or wish "that is recognized as unattainable or impermissible, the meaning being that Paul would so pray (or wish) were this permissible." C. E. B. Cranfield, *A Critical and Exegetical Commentary on the Epistle to the Romans,*

strange only to those who "love God with a covetous love, that is, because of their salvation and eternal rest or because of their escape from hell, and not for the sake of God Himself, but for their own sakes."[25] More strongly still, Luther says those who "truly love God with a filial love and friendship" will "freely offer themselves to the entire will of God, even to hell and eternal death, if that is what God wills, so that His will may be fully done. Therefore they seek absolutely nothing for themselves."[26]

Luther seems here to think of love solely in terms of an agreement of wills but not at all in terms of a desire for union or co-presence. Thus, if God condemns me to eternal separation from his presence, so long as I concur in that condemnation, I love God rightly. Indeed, were I unwilling to concur in it, my love would be impure and, presumably, selfish. But this is to want to be something more self-sufficient than God's creature; for desire for God is (as Nygren himself allows) the mark of the creature. To renounce even desire for the vision of God is to renounce our creatureliness — which is the primal sin.

The desire to make one's love of God "pure" can easily become a motive or strategy for trying to be certain that one has pleased God. The focus of love then subtly shifts from the beloved to the self. Contrary to the intention of Luther's theology, assurance of our standing before God then requires ever deeper introspection into the purity of our love. "No one," Luther writes, "knows whether he loves God with a pure heart unless he has experienced in himself that if it should please God he would not desire even to be saved nor would he refuse to be

vol. 2, International Critical Commentary (Edinburgh: T. & T. Clark, 1979), pp. 455-56.

25. Martin Luther, *Lectures on Romans, Glosses and Scholia,* in *Luther's Works,* vol. 25 (St. Louis: Concordia, 1972), pp. 380-81.

26. Luther, *Lectures on Romans,* p. 381.

damned."[27] This idea of "resignation to damnation" is not, of course, original with Luther; he had inherited a concern for "pure love" from elements of the medieval tradition.[28] Moreover, at least according to Paul Althaus, "Luther does not explicitly repeat this thought in his later writings."[29] Nevertheless, of such an idea, wherever it appears in Christian thought, I think we must finally agree with the judgment of Kenneth Kirk:

> To *refuse* to think of reward, to set oneself deliberately to *ignore* the idea of reward, is as unevangelical, though not as immoral, as to practice virtue for the sake of reward. It is as much a quest for merit as the most mercenary bargaining with God. . . . It turns the mind from God, and forces it back upon the self and its own successes and failures. *As a practical maxim for life,* the phrase, "The first concern of ethical thought should be for the purity of moral motive," is a profoundly dangerous guide.[30]

For, after all, to seek God is to seek the happy life.

To Seek the Happy Life Is to Seek God:
An Amorphous Quest?

In Augustine's quest for the happy life — which turned out to be a search for that God who, in the Word made flesh, came

27. Luther, *Lectures on Romans*, p. 381.

28. Cf., for example, Kirk, lecture VIII, part III ("Disinterestedness and Pure Love").

29. Paul Althaus, *The Theology of Martin Luther* (Philadelphia: Fortress, 1966), p. 286.

30. Kirk, p. 145.

unto his own, emptied himself, and died for the ungodly (*Conf.* 7.9) — he had companions. He tells us in book 6 that his friend Nebridius also "burned to discover the happy life," and he writes of his "great friend" Alypius, that "together with me he was in a state of mental confusion as to what way of life we should take" (6.10). "I was," Augustine writes, "in love with the idea of the happy life, but I feared to find it in its true place, and I sought for it by running away from it" (6.11).

There is, to be sure, something puzzling about this longing for the happy life, which so many share, and Augustine exploits these baffling possibilities fully in his short discussion in book 10 (20-23). On the one hand he is confident that if all people were "asked with one voice: 'Do you wish to be happy?' they would without any doubt reply, 'We do'" (10.20). Yet, those who look for happiness anywhere other than in God are actually seeking what cannot bring happiness. Hence, they seem to be both seeking and not seeking happiness. "So it is not certain that all men want to be happy" (10.23). In the early stages of his search, Augustine's quest for the happy life had hardly even seemed to be a quest for God. "I did not know how to love you" (4.2). Later, as his problem is described less in cognitive and more in volitional terms, his loves are simply too divided. He wants to be happy, yet he cannot rest in the One he himself believes will answer the longing of his heart. Those who look elsewhere than to God can in one sense hardly be said to want the happy life. But maybe they do — maybe they both want and do not want it, as that single individual Augustine had both willed and been unwilling to enter the service of the Lord (8.10).

It is worth noting that this puzzle — how it could be that all seek the happy life, which can only be found in God, but all do not seem to know or seek God — preoccupied Augustine from beginning to end. Thus, in the early *Soliloquies* he could write of "God, who art loved, wittingly or unwittingly, by everything that is capable of loving" (*Solil.* 1.2). The idea of such (witting or unwitting) love grew only more baffling, and we might say that one purpose of Augustine's great work *On the Trinity* is to explore how we can love someone (God) we do not know. "Something can be known and not loved; what I am asking is whether something can be loved which is unknown" (*Trin.* 8.3). Augustine is certain that "[w]hat you are absolutely ignorant of you simply cannot love in any sense whatever" (10.1). The answer, at least in part for Augustine, is to "[e]mbrace love which is God, and embrace God with love. . . . And if a man is full of love, what is he full of but God?" (8.6) — an assertion Andrew Louth has called "one of Augustine's boldest claims."[31]

This sense — that all who embrace love are seeking God, whether they know it or not — is what led Nygren to assert that Augustine's conversion "produced no essential change."[32] That is, the quest was still the same old acquisitive one, and the postconversion Augustine had simply found an object that better satisfied his desire. Nothing essentially new or different had happened. Augustine's quest remained the same because it was the same quest on which all who desire their happiness embark. Nygren seems to assume, of course, that a changed object of love — even a turn to God as the object of one's love — in no way transforms the quest itself, an assumption we may eventually want to question.

In one sense there need be nothing terribly puzzling about desiring happiness while being uncertain what object will sat-

31. Andrew Louth, "Love and the Trinity: Saint Augustine and the Greek Fathers," *Augustinian Studies* 33, no. 1 (2002): 6.
32. Nygren, p. 465.

isfy the desire; indeed, every adolescent knows the feeling. Augustine notes at one point that he had dedicated his first books (the no-longer-extant books on "The Beautiful and the Fitting") to Hiereus, a famous orator at Rome. "I had never seen the man, but I had come to love him because of his very great reputation for learning." Augustine knew of him from his many admirers, who praised him as a master rhetorician and philosopher. "So he was praised and, without ever having been seen, was loved" (*Conf.* 4.14). This is not so unlike the heart's longing for *eudaimonia* — for a happiness that is praised but cannot be precisely identified.

Nevertheless, if to seek the happy life is (really) to seek God, and if all seek that happy life, then it would seem that every religious quest is fundamentally the same. As Vergil says to Dante, all seek the same fruit, though they seek it on many different boughs. And, in turn, God is understood less in particular terms (as the God revealed in the Word made flesh) than in general terms (as the One who satisfies the inherent longing of the human heart). God is defined less in terms of the revelation to Israel and in Jesus, more in terms of human desire. To suppose that seeking the happy life is seeking God gives us an Augustine who opens the door to Feuerbach (God as the projection of our self-alienation) or Freud (God as the product of human wish-fulfillment). A God defined as one who must answer our felt desire for happiness is a God defined in our terms, after our own image. The longing for the happy life that is (really) love for God is, then, simply built into our nature. It is, in Oliver O'Donovan's words, "a kind of dynamic nostalgia rather than a transcendent summons from the center."[33]

---

33. Oliver O'Donovan, *The Problem of Self-Love in St. Augustine* (New Haven and London: Yale University Press, 1980), p. 157.

Even a traditional and orthodox Christian theology risks falling into the hands of Feuerbach or Freud if it attempts to subsume the whole of theology into soteriology. Thus, for example, we might easily misuse Melanchthon's formula that to know Christ is to know his benefits. He writes in article IV of the Apology of the Augsburg Confession: "This is how God wants to become known and worshiped, namely, that we receive blessings from him, and indeed, that we receive them on account of his mercy and not on account of our own merits" (¶60). Luther's well-known words in the explication of the first commandment in his Large Catechism are, as always, still more forceful: "A 'god' is the term for that to which we are to look for all good and in which we are to find refuge in all need." Both Melanchthon and Luther are emphasizing the truth that we know God as he truly is only when, seeing him revealed in the person of Christ, we are assured of his favor toward us. Accurate as that is, a theology developed with only that soteriological concern in mind can all too easily fall into the trap — quite contrary to its actual intent — of defining God in terms of our desire ("that to which we are to look for all good").

How complex this is can be seen from Karl Barth's sideways glance at Melanchthon in Barth's discussion of how Christians are to praise and thank God for his benefits. "Thanks is not just the acknowledgment of received and expected gifts; it must also be an honoring of God for his own sake. It is thanks for God's benefits; it becomes thanks for his beneficence; it finally becomes thanks for the existence of God as the Benefactor and his acknowledgment as such."[34] In the context of this movement from benefits to beneficence to Benefactor, Barth

34. Karl Barth, *The Christian Life* (Grand Rapids: Eerdmans, 1981), p. 87.

thinks of Melanchthon: "In a less happy moment Melanchthon (*Loci Communes*, 1521) emphasized the benefits of Christ
instead of Christ himself as the incarnate Logos of the eternal
Father. Various movements in modern Protestant theology
have praised him for this. But it has had the result that in Prot-
estantism praise of the divine Benefactor has become a very
feeble matter, relevant at most only in poetry."[35]

It is at least a partial answer to such worries to note that, if
in our search for the happy life we really find God, we may
learn better. The nature of the quest itself may be transformed.
Thus, for example, in *Surprised by Joy* Lewis notes, "I had
hoped that the heart of reality might be of such a kind that we
can best symbolize it as a place; instead, I found it to be a person. For all I knew, the total rejection of what I called Joy might
be one of the demands, might be the very first demand, He
would make upon me."[36] Indeed, a person carries the harsh,
resistant quality of reality — resistant, that is, to our desires
and purposes. What Lewis learned is that "God is to be obeyed
because of what He is in Himself. If you ask why we should
obey God, in the last resort the answer is, 'I am.'"[37] Augustine
learned essentially the same lesson: "All ask what they wish,
but they do not always hear what they want to hear. He serves
you best who is not so anxious to hear from you what he wills
as to will what he hears from you" (*Conf.* 10.26).

The larger issue raised by Augustine's belief that to seek the
happy life is to seek God is one that can helpfully be framed in
terms George Lindbeck has made well known. Lindbeck distinguished between "experiential-expressive" and "cultural-

35. Barth, p. 87.
36. Lewis, *Surprised by Joy*, p. 230.
37. Lewis, *Surprised by Joy*, p. 231.

linguistic" models of religion.[38] The experiential-expressive model is not unlike Augustine's depiction of the restless human heart. It posits a core human experience — unthematized or unarticulated — like a longing for the happy life. This core experience may come to expression in different ways among different people and cultures. Whether articulated as a desire for happiness, a sense of absolute dependence, or an experience of ultimate concern, it is a search that is subjectively the same. In far less sophisticated ways, the countless "spiritualities" that currently thrive in our culture may be different expressions of the same yearning.[39] If the Bible's story of Israel and Jesus speaks to such people, that will be because it seems to provide what they were already seeking. They know their story, and now they find it in the Bible. But, of course, they might also find their story in the Gita. No matter, since the core experience, the fundamental longing, is the same.

If the experiential-expressive model begins with an inner experience and moves outward toward some object or belief system that seems to offer an answer apposite to the experience, the cultural-linguistic model reverses that direction of movement. Indeed, one can make this point even more strongly, as Lindbeck does. "Instead of deriving external features of a religion from inner experience, it is the inner experiences which are viewed as derivative."[40] One moves from outside in. Without the categories, symbols, and stories that a

38. George Lindbeck, *The Nature of Doctrine* (Philadelphia: Westminster, 1984). See especially chap. 2.

39. Thus Lindbeck writes of the "multitudes of men and women who are impelled, if they have religious yearnings, to embark on their own individual quests for symbols of transcendence. The churches have become purveyors of this commodity rather than communities that socialize their members into coherent and comprehensive religious outlooks and forms of life" (p. 126).

40. Lindbeck, p. 34.

religion provides, we may not even be able to have certain thoughts or experience certain desires; for, Lindbeck says, "it is necessary to have the means for expressing an experience in order to have it."[41] And those whose categories, symbols, and stories differ will of necessity have different religious experiences. We are not all engaged in the same religious quest. From this perspective the truth is not that believers find their story in the Bible, but rather that they learn to make the Bible's story their own — to think in the terms it provides. If they look to the God revealed in Jesus for happiness, that will be because this story has taught them to think of human beings as made for fellowship with that God, from whom they are alienated by sin. Perhaps, the cultural-linguistic model might suggest, Augustine's story of the restless heart is less the generic human story than the story of one who had already drunk in Christian faith with Monica's milk.

These philosophical and theological issues perplex Christians anytime they try to speak of their faith to those who do not share it. Shall we attempt to "translate" the Christian faith into terms that make sense to our hearers, terms drawn from their cultural context? Or shall we simply tell them the story of Israel and Jesus, as straightforwardly as possible, assuming that the story is able to make its way into their lives? No doubt we generally do a little of each. And, in fact, these issues come directly to the fore in what might at first seem like the very down-to-earth and unphilosophical task of translation — as, for example, in any attempt to translate the Bible into the language of a different culture. Translators sometimes aim at a translation that will

---

41. Lindbeck, p. 37. This is obviously akin to the philosophical claim that a private language is impossible and, like that claim, is unlikely to capture the full truth of human experience.

achieve in the new language an "equivalent effect" or "semantic equivalence," and that is surely necessary to some extent. Still, one might think that the conversion of a speaker (or a group of speakers) must also involve, finally, the conversion and transformation of the speaker's language. Movement takes place in both directions. On the one hand, as Christ becomes incarnate in human flesh, so Christian faith takes on the flesh and bones of a new language and seeks to have its equivalent effect in that language. On the other hand, as Christ is crucified and risen, so also the language of new believers must undergo its own restructuring and transformation.

Or perhaps the contrast is, finally, too sharp. After all, the Augustine who wrote the *Confessions* went on eventually to write the *City of God* as well, and if there were ever a work in which — to use Lindbeck's arresting phrase — the scriptural world absorbed the universe, *City of God* might be that book.[42] And it turns out that learning to think within the contours of the Bible's story gives us — or at least gave Augustine — reason to anticipate that even those who had not learned to think in the terms of that story were engaged in an inchoate search for happiness that would be, if fully articulated and realized, a search for God. If we really learn to think of life in the terms the Bible provides, we will anticipate that even those who do not know its story, but are made for the God from whom they are separated, must desire a happiness whose object and content they can scarcely articulate. This does not mean they will necessarily ever find the One for whom they long, but it does mean that in seeking the happy life they seek God. Hence, although the theme of the restless heart provides no apologetic argument by which Christians can persuade others to believe, it does shape

42. Lindbeck, p. 117.

an anticipation and suggest an invitation. It anticipates an un-fulfilled longing for rest, and it invites one to turn, as Augus-tine eventually did, to "the food that is incorruptible" (*Conf.* 3.1).

Just when we persuade ourselves, however, that it is reason-able to assert that all people desire to rest in God (at least in the sense that they long for a happiness that can come only from looking to God), we may encounter a very different challenge to this assertion. One might argue that such a claim is (at best) unpersuasive and (at worst) condescending to those who claim to experience no desire for God. As Hans Blumenberg has ar-gued forcefully, it may ignore or conceal modernity's claim to have made a radically new beginning based not on revelation but on reason or science.

> Any historical self-consciousness that believed itself capa-ble of making, or believed it had already made, another new beginning, a beginning that was supposed to consti-tute a "modern age" . . . as a scientifically grounded and therefore final epoch, was bound to come into conflict with this Christian claim to novelty and finality. The final-ity in the Christian self-conception was bound to try to as-sert itself against this by denying the possible authenticity of any such founding act in history and at the same time accusing it of having had to make illegitimate use of the truth that belongs to Christianity.[43]

Hence, according to Blumenberg, modernity is not a distor-tion or corruption of Christianity; it is an innovative rational project in its own right. If it sometimes inevitably seems to ad-

---

43. Hans Blumenberg, *The Legitimacy of the Modern Age* (Cambridge: MIT Press, 1985), p. 74.

dress a question or to speak in language that is continuous with — or at least left over from — an era of Christian belief, that is to be expected and should not be taken as an indication that Augustine's story of the restless heart longing for God is "really" the story of "Everyman."

To the degree that we grant some legitimacy to Blumenberg's argument — and, hence, to the modern age — we will simply have recognized that in modernity's assertion of human autonomy and Christianity's assertion that a universal longing for happiness can be fulfilled only by looking to God, we have contrasting and opposing patterns of thought and speech, which will be rivals for our assent and commitment. In hearts that acknowledge no antecedent desire for God, the gospel will still make its own way. But at least from the other side of Christian commitment we will learn to tell our story as the story of those who, even if unwittingly, desire the God for whom we are made — and we will anticipate that this is true of all people, even as we realize that it may seem reasonable only to those who have begun to be shaped by the Christian story. We are, I think, saved from condescension so long as we do not insist that any desire for fulfillment on the part of moderns (who profess no longing for God) is just a secularized version of Christian desire for God — so long as we understand the Augustinian claim that all who seek the happy life seek God as less an argument than an invitation. Blumenberg's moderns will have to see whether a story that does not look to God for our happiness, an autonomy that is its own ground and that desires to offer no praise, can finally keep them safe — not from our arguments but from the invitation of the God who nonetheless claims them as his own. For that God, as Augustine says, resists the proud.

Hence, Christians affirm that the God who cannot be found

apart from the Word made flesh does not come as a stranger in that incarnate Word. He comes to "his own" (John 1:11), to those whose longing for the happy life must, if it is to be satisfied, look to him. And his coming in the Word made flesh is not unmotivated; it is the fruit of his desire to reclaim humanity as the object of his love. If Augustine's view of the quest for the happy life is in a sense amorphously anthropocentric, it is so because the biblical narrative has authorized him to anticipate from the human heart an unthematized longing planted in the depths of our created nature. When we come to believe that it is God for whom we have been looking and that in embracing the longing that is love we are embracing God, when false or partial answers reveal their poverty, then that true Object of desire will differ from our substitutes "not as white from black but as a perfect circle from a child's first attempt to draw a wheel. But when the child has learned to draw, it will know that the circle it then makes is what it was trying to make from the very beginning."[44]

If this is the right way to think with Augustine, we can begin to see what went wrong in Anders Nygren's masterful work *Agape and Eros*. For Nygren it is imperative that agape be entirely "unmotivated." It answers to no need, has no rationale or presupposition. It is simply sheer, inexplicable grace. Indeed, from this perspective Nygren's account depicts human beings who are more like Blumenberg's moderns than Augustine's needy creatures. Yet, if the gospel is the message of God's agape, Nygren's understanding of agape would seem to mean that the gospel is simply an announcement of God's good favor to those who have no particular reason to desire such favor. The gospel would simply be "news" — not "good

---

44. C. S. Lewis, *The Problem of Pain* (New York: Macmillan, 1962), p. 39.

news" for those longing to hear it or an invitation to find in it that which they desire. From this perspective one would have to direct toward Nygren a criticism not unlike what he directs at Marcion: "Marcion, in the end, goes beyond the idea of Agape and robs it of its real point. Marcion says 'the stranger,' where the New Testament says 'the sinner.'"[45]

At first sight one might suppose that Nygren's mistake is that he lacks a doctrine of creation depicting the creature's need for God. Understandable as that characterization might be, O'Donovan may come closer to the truth in suggesting that Nygren's problem is that he has nothing other than a doctrine of creation. That is to say, God's redemptive work takes place against no background. Every act of God in relation to us must be a new creation. "The heart of the quarrel between Augustine and his critics, then [and, in a sense, between Augustine and Blumenberg's moderns], is whether the creative work of God allows for teleology, and so for a movement within creation, which can presuppose the fact of creation as a given starting point, to a destiny which 'fulfills' creation by redeeming it and lifting it to a new level."[46]

To acknowledge the inchoate and unthematized longing, which all have, as a desire for God is not to underplay the revelation of the grace of God as, in O'Donovan's words quoted earlier, "a transcendent summons from the center."[47] On the contrary, it is simply to acknowledge that God always takes the initiative with us and that it is his gift when we come to know what we desire. "Because our turning toward happiness is a blind seeking," Josef Pieper writes, "we are, whenever happi-

45. Nygren, p. 326.
46. O'Donovan, p. 158.
47. O'Donovan, p. 157.

ness comes our way, the recipients of something unforeseen, something unforeseeable, and therefore not subject to planning and intention. Happiness is essentially a gift; we are not the forgers of our own felicity."[48] Only as receivers of such a gift will we finally understand how it can be that to seek the happy life is to seek God.

Loving God with a Whole Heart:
A Totalitarian Quest?

I noted earlier that when we try to think with Augustine about what it means to seek our happiness in God, we may fear that the quest is a selfish one. Then, trying to guard against such selfishness, against the dangers of eudaimonism, we may come close to obliterating the self, which cannot be acceptable. It would, after all, be prideful self-sufficiency for one who is God's creature to repress the heart's desire for God. A careful, chastened appreciation of our need and longing for God seeks to reject both selfishness and self-sufficiency — but not the self or the desire for God that constitutes it. But now a different danger may confront us. If Augustine's eudaimonism does not obliterate but rather vindicates the self who longs for God, it has sometimes been taken to obliterate the neighbor — all those people, other than God, whom we are commanded to love. After all, if God alone satisfies the heart's longing, we may be hard pressed to explain why a heart that rests in God should have need of any other to love. There are certainly moments — many moments — in the *Confessions* when Augus-

48. Josef Pieper, *Happiness and Contemplation* (South Bend, Ind.: St. Augustine's Press, 1998), p. 25.

tine thinks he is forced to choose between love for God and love for others (in particular, of course, for a wife). The God to whom his heart is drawn, and to whom he finally turns, seems to be a totalitarian God, who leaves room for no other objects of love.

This is, of course, a very old problem; it recurs often when we try to think with Augustine about the shape of the Christian life, and I will return to it from another angle in chapter 5. Having read Cicero's *Hortensius,* Augustine finds himself "on fire to leave earthly things behind and fly back to you" (*Conf.* 3.4). Overcome by grief at the death of his friend, the young Augustine concludes that he had mistakenly "poured out my soul like water onto sand by loving a man who was bound to die just as if he were an immortal" (4.8). Loving God with a whole heart seems to drive out all other loves. So satisfying — or so overpowering — is God as the object of our love that there seems to be neither need nor room for others. Their absence can exercise no veto power over our ability to find joy and fulfillment in God.

It is, I think, a partial — but only partially satisfactory — answer to this problem to say, as I once did myself, that in finding God we find the One who gives us others to love.[49] To be sure, that belief does characterize Augustine's understanding of the Christian's earthly pilgrimage. Along our path of life, God gives us others to love. They serve as a kind of "school" in which we learn the real meaning of love, and they draw us out beyond themselves as we gradually learn to love not just the gift but also the Giver. The danger that we may think of others, then, simply as rungs on the ladder by which we ascend to the

---

49. Gilbert Meilaender, *Friendship: A Study in Theological Ethics* (Notre Dame, Ind.: University of Notre Dame Press, 1981), pp. 18-19.

love of God is forestalled by the sense that when we find God, we find One who continues to give us others as objects of our love, who are not to be left behind. There is, as I said, something to this move, but it works best when applied to the course of earthly life, during which an unsatisfied longing remains as an inevitable component of our love for God. But what about heaven? What happens when the longing for God is perfectly satisfied and the lover rests in God? What else could one need at that point? For, as Augustine puts it in *City of God* (22.30), in heaven we will experience "the delight of eternal joys, forgetting all offences, forgetting all punishments." And, one might wonder, forgetting friends and loved ones left behind? Would needing anything else suggest that the experienced presence of God was somehow an insufficient answer to the longing of the human heart?

Martha Nussbaum has recently reopened this enduring problem in an essay entitled "Augustine and Dante on the Ascent of Love." Would a Christian whose love for God was gradually growing toward perfection have, concomitantly, increasingly less need to rest any of the heart's longing in other human beings? Nussbaum suggests that, though Augustine may have believed after his conversion that an increasingly perfected love of God (or the Good) would be increasingly self-sufficient — serene, invulnerable, and in need of no other good — he did not for long hold such a view. By the time we get to the Augustine of the *Confessions,* he has come to believe that such self-sufficiency is neither attainable nor (even were it attainable) desirable in this life.

The last of these claims is the really interesting one — that self-sufficiency would not be desirable in this life, even were it attainable. The problem is not simply that old habits of sin cling more unrelentingly than Augustine might once have supposed. More fundamental is the fact that a "goal of God-like self-sufficiency is now seen by Augustine as a form of deep impiety. . . . Openness, waiting, longing, groaning become forms of worship and acknowledgment."[50] We wait on God — waiting for the grace of God by which alone our love is made secure, and which can happen not in this life but only in the next. This is, as Nussbaum notes, the kind of love for God that Augustine depicts in the *Confessions*. In particular, in book 10 he surely does not depict the believer's earthly pilgrimage as a life marked by increasing serenity or contentment. Instead, taking stock of his progress in love, Augustine is forced to admit that in certain crucial respects he simply cannot tell whether his love for God is gradually growing toward perfection. "In this matter I know less of myself than of you" (10.37). The prayer that becomes a powerful refrain in book 10 — "Give what you command, and command what you will" — is a confession of the insufficiency and neediness that always characterize earthly life. If the longing for God is to be satisfied, if Augustine is to rest in God, it will not be in this life. Here and now the heart still clings to earthly loves and, inevitably therefore, is vulnerable, experiencing loss and sorrow.

The full implications of this picture of earthly life as radically incomplete come to clear articulation in *City of God*, where, as Nussbaum puts it, "the entirety of the ancient eudaimonist project is now denounced as infected by pride."[51] The point is made yet more strikingly by Peter Brown. Referring to the opening chapters of book 19 of *City of God*, in which Augustine — drawing on Varro — considers classical

50. Martha Nussbaum, "Augustine and Dante on the Ascent of Love," in *The Augustinian Tradition*, ed. Gareth B. Matthews (Berkeley, Los Angeles, and London: University of California Press, 1999), pp. 61-90, here p. 69.

51. Nussbaum, p. 70.

theories of the good life, Brown writes that "by enumerating and rejecting the 288 possible ethical theories known to Marcus Varro . . . Augustine marks the end of classical thought."[52] Even at its very best, this life, Augustine believes, is "weighed down by such great and grievous ills, or at the mercy of such chances," that it "would never be called happy." On the contrary, the highest good cannot be enjoyed "in this condition of mortality" (19.4). Even when we achieve some virtue and enact love for the good, this is always done in the midst of "internal strife," divided as the heart is between virtue and vice. And however great an achievement such action may be, those whose lives are still characterized by internal struggle can hardly be said to rest in the Good. Christians must therefore live in hope, not yet possessing a present salvation (19.4).

Already in book 14 Augustine had rejected any attempt to remove from Christian life the emotions and passions that make us vulnerable, needy, and incomplete beings. Not to feel grief at one's sins and shortcomings would, for example, not be moral progress. To imagine that the heart's longing could be satisfied by a state free of passion would mean that "love and gladness" could have no place in "the final complete happiness" (14.9). Not to seek our happiness in some good outside ourselves — even if thereby we risk pain and loss — would be a mark of sin. If, here and now, we felt none of the emotions that arise within a life given over to love of neighbors, "there would really be something wrong with our life." To be free from any longings — the longings that make us needy, dependent, and vulnerable — would not be a moral achievement,

52. P. R. L. Brown, "Saint Augustine and Political Society," in *The City of God: A Collection of Critical Essays*, ed. Dorothy F. Donnelly (New York: Peter Lang, 1995), p. 26.

nor would it give "true tranquillity." On the contrary, it would be a "monstrous" state, from which was missing "every shred of humanity" (14.9). To repeat: Augustine does not conclude that the classical search for the self-sufficient life is misguided only because it is unattainable in temporal life. He concludes that attaining it would be a step not toward but away from God, away from admitting that the human heart could not be at rest except in God. Hence, there is something to Nussbaum's suggestion that "the diseased swollen earthly city is closer to God, because more passionate, more willing to turn outward and to search for an adequate object, than the torporous city of the Stoic wise man, wrapped in its own fatal pride."[53]

In his preface to the paperback edition of *The Screwtape Letters*, C. S. Lewis writes of "the ruthless, sleepless, unsmiling concentration upon self which is the mark of Hell."[54] It is in fact that concentration upon self, not longing for God, that ultimately obliterates the person of the neighbor. Lewis reminds the reader of Milton's "devil with devil damned Firm concord holds," and comments: "But how? . . . A being which can still love is not yet a devil."[55] This is the truth in Nussbaum's claim that (for Augustine) "the diseased swollen earthly city is closer to God" than a city in which each person is turned inward in search of self-sufficiency and invulnerability (though there is no guarantee that the "passionate" city will find its fulfillment in God and, thus, become something other than just a version of the earthly city). To be sure, burdened as we are with disordered earthly loves, we are not yet prepared to love God with a whole heart. But we are at least looking outward, still in search

53. Nussbaum, pp. 70-71.
54. C. S. Lewis, *The Screwtape Letters* (New York: Macmillan, 1961), p. ix.
55. Lewis, *The Screwtape Letters*, p. x.

of an object that can really satisfy our longing — still open to
the God who is the answer to our heart's desire.

Nussbaum is, therefore, quite prepared to defend Augustine against any claim that he remains committed to a Platonic
movement of ascent, in which the closer we come to love of the
Good, the more the neighbor (who is loved along the way) is
obliterated as a possible object of love. Much of her defense depends, in fact, on our seeing how Augustine's depiction of
Christian life has changed by the time he writes the *Confessions*. "The metaphor of ascent still appears, but rarely. In its
place we tend to find the image of a journey that goes on and
on."[56] Although it is true that we find happiness only if our
love finally rests in God, our loves are one, and there is no
jumping ahead to the end of the story. Here and now we are
given others to love, and in loving them we hold open in ourselves the gap that only God can fill, the wound that only God
can heal. Here and now we accept the incompleteness and vulnerability that love brings in its wake. Here and now, "to live in
that mystery and that openness of expectation is . . . the good
life for a human being."[57]

Here and now. But in heaven, Nussbaum argues, the love
that Augustine describes is dependent on only one object outside the self: God. Once the heart rests with assurance in God,
"there is no need, really, of other human individuals, and, it
would seem, no continued erotic vulnerability of any sort. . . .
For there is no room for loss or grief in salvation. Joy is assured for all eternity."[58] And without any possibility of loss,
there is a sense in which each lover of God might be said to en-

56. Nussbaum, p. 71.
57. Nussbaum, p. 73.
58. Nussbaum, p. 84.

joy a rest in God that is entirely independent of all others. These others are obliterated — *if* the fact that their absence would be powerless to destroy one's joy means, in essence, the obliteration of the significance of their presence.

Precisely that Nussbaum finds objectionable in Augustine's view of love. (And the point is exactly that: she is offended by his view. She does not argue that Augustine is wrong. He offends not her reason but her will.) To what exactly does she object? The point is made most clearly, perhaps, in her discussion of Dante, though the objection certainly applies with at least as much force to Augustine. "Beatrice loves Dante: but she is perfectly prepared to see him go to hell if he proves resistant to her reprimand."[59] Surely Augustine believes something similar. "When," he writes in the *Confessions,* "I shall cling to you united, I shall find no sorrow anywhere, no labor; wholly alive will my life be all full of you" (10.28). More strongly still, he contends in *City of God* that "the final complete happiness will be exempt from the spasms of fear and from any kind of grief" (14.9). Secure in God, this love is no longer vulnerable or threatened by loss.

To that Nussbaum objects. She has noted how for Augustine all our loves are of a piece and — since in this life we live in hope rather than in possession of joy — we can never really become invulnerable to loss. There is no self-sufficiency here and now, because we are drawn out of ourselves in love for both God and our neighbors. Our happiness depends on both objects of love, and therefore others must not be obliterated. Nor will we be self-sufficient there and then, when we rest in God in heaven. Our happiness will still be dependent on God — *but no longer dependent on any others.* Contemplating the hy-

59. Nussbaum, p. 83.

pothetical fact that Beatrice's heavenly joy could not be diminished were Dante not there to share it, Nussbaum asks whether such love is really love. What she is really asking, however, is whether we would — or should — want to inhabit a world in which there is an object of love such as Augustine's God, who is wholly our sufficiency. Or would a world like Dido's, in which she takes her own life in grief over her abandonment by Aeneas, be a better world, because it would be free of a totalitarian God who refuses to allow any of us a veto over the happiness of others?

It is worth our noting that Augustine answered this question — for himself — in his description in *City of God* of the sin of our first parents. Having been deceived by the serpent, Eve invited Adam to share in her sin. Adam, Augustine thinks, was not deceived. Why, then, did he too sin? Because he "refused to be separated from his only companion, even if it involved sharing her sin" (14.11). There is a seeming nobility in such refusal, and precisely that nobility attracts Nussbaum. But it is still a nobility that wants to determine the conditions of one's own happiness (even if a happiness intermingled with sorrow and vulnerability). It is therefore what Augustine calls sinful pride, and if he is right, it must end not with the fragile goodness of a vulnerable *love,* but where pride always ends: with an *isolated* self who seeks to be the author of the conditions of its own happiness. If Augustine is right, it is this assertion of self, not a longing for God, that finally obliterates the other.

None of us is permitted veto power over the happiness of others in heaven, for in the presence of God there must be fullness of joy. But Augustine can believe this without supposing that the presence of others is unimportant or adds nothing to one's joy. Each shares his own vision of God with others, thereby enriching the vision of all; for, as Augustine writes in the *Confessions*, "when many people rejoice together, the joy of each individual is all the richer, since each one inflames the other and the warmth spreads throughout them all" (8.4). Moreover, the God who draws us to himself and who is alone our sufficiency is never a tyrant who seeks to obliterate all other objects of our love. To turn in love toward that God is to turn toward One in whom we are given others to love. But they are — always and only — loved "in God"; for, apart from that location they can never truly be themselves.

When in the *Paradiso* Dante finally comes face-to-face with Beatrice, when his longing to see her has brought him to where one sees God, she then returns to her place within the heavenly ranks — smiling once more at him, and, then, turning her face to "the eternal fountain." The austerity of the moment is overpowering, and of course one might — as Nussbaum does — find that austerity offensive. But Beatrice does not leave Dante; rather, together they are to gaze at the love that moves the sun and the other stars. In God they are given back to each other, that each may enrich the vision of the other. Augustine sees — and bends the knee before — a similar truth, a vision of that God who continually gives us the neighbor to love. Recalling in the *Confessions* the death of his close friend Nebridius, Augustine writes that Nebridius now lives "in the bosom of Abraham" — whatever, as Augustine characteristically adds, that may mean. "Now he no longer turns his ear to my lips; he turns his own spiritual lips to your fountain and drinks his fill of all the wisdom that he can desire, happy without end. And I do not think that he is so inebriated with that wisdom as to forget me; since it is of you, Lord, that he drinks, and you are mindful of us" (9.3).

DUTY

THERE IS a card game called Rage, just complicated enough and just simple enough to be enjoyable for parents and their children to play together. I happen to enjoy it a lot, and over the years it is probably the game I have most often proposed that our family play together. My wife, being the cooperative soul that she is, has often acquiesced and played it, even though she does not much care for it. And it's apparent to me that she dislikes it for one of the reasons I like it. At least according to one understanding of how the game is played, participants may practice deceit, though they will be penalized if caught.

As in many simple card games, players are required to follow the lead suit if they are able. Moreover, among the game's instructions is the following: "Illegal reneging: Players must always play cards that follow the lead suit if they can. A player may not renege by playing a card of another suit if he has a card of the lead suit. If a player is suspected of reneging, he must be challenged immediately — before the next player plays. The player challenged must then show his cards to the challenger to confirm the correctness of play. If the play was legal, the challenger gets a 10-point penalty immediately. If the play was not legal, then the challenged player gets the 10-point penalty." Within the circle of my acquaintances, however, this instruction is understood as a tacit invitation to duplicity. Our mutual understanding is that any of us may attempt to "renege," and part of the interest of the game lies precisely in detecting this when it happens or in managing to "renege" successfully.

I find this enjoyable and, indeed, engage rather recklessly in the practice of reneging — so much so, sometimes, that it becomes all too predictable and eventually useless as a tactic. My wife dislikes this feature of the game, and she can almost never bring herself to take advantage of this possibility. The rest of us count on her reluctance, of course, and it enters into our calculations. My wife and I agree that duplicity is not really wrong in this setting, since, after all, our shared understanding of what we are doing makes room for just that possibility. Yet, I have sometimes wondered whether her reluctance to (shall we say) participate energetically in this feature of the game does not suggest that something about her character is a little better than mine.

Among the forms of deceit, lying is one of the most common and has often been thought to be the most serious. Why that should be may take some clarifying, and thinking with Augustine about the wrong of lying — about how that duty stands in relation to our desires — may provide such clarity, though it can also be quite bracing. Readers of the *Confessions* may recall that among the reasons (though surely only one of several) driving Augustine's decision to alter the course of his life was reflection on the fact that advancing in his chosen career meant, for example, delivering a speech in praise of the emperor, in which speech there would be "a lot of lies," which "would be applauded by those who knew that they were lies" (6.6). And readers of his treatise *Against Lying (Contra mendacium)* will likely conclude that — whatever we say about the special circumstances of a game — Augustine thought all lying to be wrong. "One can say without exaggeration," Ernest Fortin writes, "that there is no moral principle which Augustine defended with greater vehemence" than that it is always wrong to lie.[1]

Augustine believed the desire for happiness, which he saw as a desire to rest in the enjoyment of God, cannot be joined with or sustained within a way of life that countenances deliberately asserting what we know or believe to be false. There will of course be occasions in life when lying may seem to be the best or the only way to achieve some important good. Then — in an attempt to unify the moral life, to make what is *right* to *do* cohere with what it would be *good* to *accomplish* — we will be tempted to suppose that we should lie. But thinking with Augustine about lying will challenge our attempts to unify — through our own power — this split between the right and the good. For Augustine teaches that there are duties that must be adhered to even if violating them might seem to promise better results.

Thinking with Augustine about lying will also invite us to reflect on ambiguities. From one angle Augustine will surely seem too "rigorist" and finally mistaken in his insistence that the lie is always forbidden. From another angle, even this rigorous Augustine will prove to be very sensitive to the complications and ambiguities of the moral life — so sensitive that we might wonder whether Fortin was right to claim that there was no principle on which Augustine was less willing to compromise.[2]

---

1. Ernest L. Fortin, "Augustine and the Problem of Christian Rhetoric," *Augustinian Studies* 5 (1974): 97.

2. In "Two Traditions on Lying and Deception in the Ancient Church"

Augustine on the Wrong of Lying

Augustine wrote two relatively lengthy treatises on lying. In 395, rather early in his ecclesiastical career and before he had become a bishop, he wrote *De mendacio (On Lying)*. Though not without interest in places, *De mendacio* is about as convoluted a piece of writing as one can imagine, and while it may be comforting for the rest of us to know that a writer as skilled as Augustine can produce work of this sort, it is not the most helpful place to go if one wants to think through the problem of lying.[3] A quarter-century later, probably in 420, Augustine published the other treatise, *Contra mendacium*. In his small work *Faith, Hope, and Charity*, often called simply the *Enchiridion* and published a year or two after *Contra mendacium*, Augustine also briefly treats the topic of lying — a discussion whose very brevity is helpful in alerting us to the position we should expect to be central in the treatise he composed so shortly before.[4]

In addition to its greater clarity and readability, *Contra mendacium* has the added interest of being written in response

---

(*The Thomist* 49 [1985]), Boniface Ramsey, O.P., argues that there was another tradition in the ancient church, less rigorous or absolutist, that condoned some lying. That tradition, older than Augustine, survived after Augustine chiefly in Eastern thinkers. This may be, but my suggestion that Augustine's own view makes place for a less rigorous possibility will turn not on such historical matters, but on a theological point about martyrdom.

3. John von Heyking (*Augustine and Politics as Longing in the World* [Columbia and London: University of Missouri Press, 2001], p. 115) claims that *De mendacio*, although earlier than *Contra mendacium*, is actually the better treatise, because it is more subtle and indirect. It takes a very devoted "Straussian" reader, however, to be persuaded by von Heyking's argument.

4. I will cite the translation from the Ancient Christian Writers series: St. Augustine, *Faith, Hope, and Charity*, trans. Louis A. Arand (New York and Ramsey, N.J.: Newman, 1947). Citations will be identified by chapter and page number.

to an intriguing inquiry.[5] Consentius, a pious Catholic, had written to ask Augustine whether it might be permissible to use deceptive tactics to infiltrate and undermine the heretical Priscillianist movement. Priscillian teaching had about it a Manichean flavor — advocating a rigorous asceticism, renouncing marriage, and regarding the body as enmeshed in evil. Priscillian himself was executed in 385, after which his rapidly spreading body of followers turned to secrecy. Believing that the general run of the people could not appreciate their esoteric teaching, Priscillians held that they were permitted to disguise their true beliefs — even to lie about them — in the good cause of spreading the truth as they saw it.

Wanting evidently to fight fire with fire, Consentius appears to have written Augustine to ask whether Catholics might not, in turn, lie and deceive in order to infiltrate the Priscillianist movement and expose its adherents. In one sense Augustine's answer is brief and succinct: "They [the Priscillianists] must be refuted, not imitated" (2:127). Yet, his discussion is by no means brief; indeed, it is supple and attentive to complexity. It will be worth our while, first, to sort through his most important arguments.

Even to define what we mean by lying is no easy task, and Augustine's discussion is not without its difficulties. It is clear — and, I think, relatively unproblematic — that for Augustine deception encompasses more than lying and is sometimes permissible, as is concealing the truth (by means that do not involve lying). But the forbidden lie, as Augustine writes in

5. I will cite the translation from the Fathers of the Church series: Saint Augustine, *Treatises on Various Subjects*, vol. 14, ed. Roy J. Deferrari (Washington, D.C.: Catholic University of America Press, 1952). Citations will be identified by chapter and page number. I will also cite the earlier treatise, *De mendacio*, in the same manner from this same volume.

one of his most direct formulations, "is a false signification told with desire to deceive" (12:160). The complication in this definition is that it includes an offense against truth (the false signification) and an offense against trust (the desire to deceive).[6] In a rigorous dissection of Augustine's views, though one that relies primarily on *De mendacio*, Paul Griffiths has argued that, though an intention to deceive is of course often present when one lies, what makes the lie (for Augustine) is the offense against truth: "the mismatch between what's in your heart (what you take to be true) and what's on your tongue (what you say to be true)."[7] There are others, however, who believe that offense against trust ought to be at least as great a moral concern. Thus, Bernard Williams (though not explicating Augustine) writes: "If lying is inherently an abuse of assertion [i.e., an offense against truth], then so is deliberately exploiting the way in which one's hearer can be expected to understand one's choice of assertion [i.e., abusing the hearer's trust]."[8]

I am inclined to agree with the thrust of Williams's comment. Moreover, I believe Augustine does in fact think of lies as including both "false signification" and "desire to deceive,"

6. Although the categories are not unique to his discussion — and indeed, in some ways almost impose themselves upon anyone who thinks about the wrong of lying — I believe I first drew them from Alasdair MacIntyre, "Truthfulness, Lies, and Moral Philosophers: What Can We Learn from Mill and Kant?" in *The Tanner Lectures on Human Values*, vol. 16 (Salt Lake City: University of Utah Press, 1995), pp. 309-61. Theologians sometimes make a similar point by setting the requirements of truth against the requirements of love.

7. Paul J. Griffiths, *Lying: An Augustinian Theology of Duplicity* (Grand Rapids: Brazos, 2004), p. 26.

8. Bernard Williams, *Truth and Truthfulness* (Princeton and Oxford: Princeton University Press, 2002), p. 107.

though it is not easy to hold together his several comments.[9] For example, in the *Enchiridion* he writes that "the real evil of lying" is "think[ing] one thing and say[ing] another" (6:27); yet, he also writes that "everyone who lies says the opposite of what is in his mind, and that in order to deceive" (7:32). At least one important issue does turn on what we say about this definitional issue. If we confine the wrong of lying to the offense against truth (thinking one thing and saying another), we may leave open possibilities for deceiving others — indeed, intentionally deceiving them — without lying. We retain the prohibition on lying yet find room to deceive in circumstances where it would seem wrong or unwise simply to tell the truth straightforwardly. Just such a move gives rise to the long tradition supporting equivocation (which deliberately takes advantage of the hearer's probable misunderstanding) or even "mental reservation" (which leaves unspoken various qualifications that the hearer could not possibly surmise). Suppose, for example, that while vigorously upholding an absolute prohibition on lying, I tell my neighbor, "Someone has slashed the tires on your car," omitting the fact that it was I who did this. If and when my neighbor learns the whole truth of the matter, no doubt he will have to agree that I did not lie to him. But is he likely to trust me in the future? Or to suppose that this deceit was somehow less troubling than an outright lie would have been? But this example might be skewed by the fact that it was wrong of me to slash his tires. Some may be more approving of the oft-cited story of a deception (without lying) practiced by Saint Athanasius. As Newman recounts it,

9. An additional bit of evidence: Christopher Levenick notes that Augustine clearly holds that the joke is distinct from the lie, "repeatedly citing the joke's evident lack of desire to deceive." "Augustine on Lying, Joking, and Jesting," *Augustinian Studies* 35, no. 2 (2004): 310.

Athanasius "was in a boat on the Nile, flying persecution; and he found himself pursued. On this he ordered his men to turn his boat round, and ran right to meet the satellites of Julian. They asked him, 'Have you seen Athanasius?' and he told his followers to answer, 'Yes, he is close to you.' *They* went on their course as if they were sure to come up to him, while *he* ran back into Alexandria, and there lay hid till the end of the persecution."[10] Now in such a case — a just man, let us stipulate for the moment, fleeing from men aiming to do him evil — might it be that while still eschewing entirely the lie, we could rightly speak a deliberately equivocal truth? It is hard to see why, if Athanasius may be permitted this deception, he may not also be permitted to lie. Lying speech, as Griffiths acutely notes, distorts and ruptures our humanity because it uses words simply to pursue our own purposes. "Lying speech is owned, controlled, taken charge of, characteristically and idiosyncratically yours. True speech is disowned, relinquished, returned as gift to its giver, definitively and universally not yours. . . . Lying is derived from, is a paradigmatic instance of, living according to yourself. If you try to live in this way, you attempt to live autonomously, to take your own nature and desires as your only guides for life and speech."[11] Yet, of course, the deceptive (but nonlying) words of Athanasius and his followers also seem to take control of words for their purposes. If their words are not wrong, we should at least hold open for the moment the possibility that there may also be lying words that are not claimed as our own but are given and relinquished in service of others.

10. John Henry Cardinal Newman, Appendix G, "Lying and Equivocation," in *Apologia Pro Vita Sua* (Boston: Houghton Mifflin, 1956), p. 326.
11. Griffiths, pp. 85-86.

Life will, of course, present us with many occasions when we might seem to have a good (and not merely self-serving) reason to lie. Augustine recognizes that and indeed thinks our reasons for lying make some moral difference. "Some will ask whether in view of what we have been saying any thief at all is to be ranked on a par with one who steals for the sake of mercy. Who would maintain this? . . . He who steals for lust is worse than he who steals for mercy" (C. mend. 8:145). Nevertheless, he immediately adds, if theft in every instance is a sin, then "we must abstain from all theft." And of course, he would say the same of lying. Hence, motives do count in our moral evaluations. Why a person does what he does always enters into our overall moral judgment. But were motives all that mattered, perhaps any deed, however heinous, could sometimes be justified. "Such would be the outcome if once we grant that in all the evil work of men we are not to ask what is done, but merely why it is done, so that whatever is found to have been done for good reasons is not judged to be evil in itself" (7:144).

Because an appeal to praiseworthy motives alone cannot be sufficient to justify lying, we will have to look more closely at Augustine's reasons for holding that lying is always wrong. Throughout Contra mendacium he offers a variety of arguments, but there are, I think, five that are most fundamental.

Perhaps most obvious, if only because it is where he begins in his reply to Consentius, is that there is something self-defeating about lying. "[H]ow can I suitably proceed against lies by lying?" (1:126). Augustine sees that because speech is central to the bond of human community, lying subverts that bond. As Charles Fried observes, "truth-telling seems to bear a fundamental, pervasive relation to the human enterprise, just as lying appears to be fundamentally subversive of that enterprise."[12] Hence, Fried notes, in words reminiscent of Griffiths's suggestion that lying speech is evidence of an attempt to own and control what is not ours, when we lie we enact a "kind of treachery" — taking something held in common, something intended to bind human beings together, and using it for our own private purposes. "This much I know," Augustine writes, "that even he who teaches that we ought to lie wants to appear to be teaching the truth" (18:173). Without some reliance on what others say, not only community but even communication would break down. How self-defeating the lie may be Augustine sees when contemplating one possible result of what Consentius has in mind. Suppose the Priscillianists, under pressure, give up their false views. It is not, Augustine points out, "clear how we shall be in a position to trust as converted the men to whom we lied when perverted" (3:133). And again, "Do you not see whither this evil tends? It tends not only to make us appear suspect to them and them to us, but it tends, and not without cause, to make every brother appear suspect to every brother" (4:134).

This is a powerful argument; yet, we might well doubt whether it is sufficient to persuade us that all lying is wrong. It might be, after all, that isolated instances of lying for good reason would not really undermine the bond of human life in community and might even serve to sustain it. Certainly there are occasions when it takes a considerable effort to believe otherwise. Therefore, alongside the claim that lying speech undermines human community, we should place an argument that focuses less on those to whom the lie is spoken and more on the one who lies. We do something to ourself, to our char-

---

12. Charles Fried, *Right and Wrong* (Cambridge, Mass., and London: Harvard University Press, 1978), p. 61.

acter, when we lie — or so Augustine thinks. Thus, even if a lie in no way harms the one who is deceived, "it is harmful to the liar to have wanted to deceive" (3:129-30). This is in part because of the all-too-well-known fact that one lie tends to beget the need for another and still another. We may find that "little by little and bit by bit this evil will grow" until it becomes "a mass of wicked lies" (18:172).

A powerful example of how one might become embedded or enmeshed in a world of untruth is expressed in "After Ten Years," a "reckoning" composed by Dietrich Bonhoeffer for his fellow conspirators. A brief, haunting paragraph — titled "Are We Still of Any Use?" — captures well the sense that a willingness to lie even in a good cause may recoil upon the liar, turning him into what he did not intend.

> We have been silent witnesses of evil deeds; we have been drenched by many storms; we have learnt the arts of equivocation and pretence; experience has made us suspicious of others and kept us from being truthful and open; intolerable conflicts have worn us down and even made us cynical. Are we still of any use? What we shall need is not geniuses, or cynics, or misanthropes, or clever tacticians, but plain, honest, straightforward men. Will our inward power of resistance be strong enough, and our honesty with ourselves remorseless enough, for us to find our way back to simplicity and straightforwardness?[13]

What we say in words — which might seem merely an external matter — turns in upon us and shapes the persons we be-

---

13. Dietrich Bonhoeffer, *Letters and Papers from Prison* (New York: Macmillan, 1972), p. 16.

come. It is because a willingness to lie can turn us into people who *are* liars that I wondered at the outset of this chapter whether my wife's reluctance to lie even in a game might not indicate that her character was better formed than mine.

But perhaps not. Granting the force of Augustine's argument, and granting the power of Bonhoeffer's example, one might still argue that the way out of being trapped within a web of lies that leaves no road back to simplicity and straightforwardness is — assuming the goodness of a cause such as Bonhoeffer's — to break free of the sense that lying in such a good cause somehow taints or defiles us. If it is right to do, how can it be harmful to one's character? Perhaps a rather more robust conscience is needed. Thus, Bernard Williams writes that "if it is right to lie [for some important good], . . . it is no sign of a good disposition to feel bad about it."[14] Larry Rasmussen's critique of the resistance movement of Bonhoeffer and his coconspirators offers a kind of empirical support for Williams's claim. Rasmussen asks why the resistance movement turned out to be such a tactical failure, which need not necessarily have been the case. His answer, in part, is that "nice fellows do not make good revolutionaries."[15] By this he means that Bonhoeffer and the others were led by their philosophical and theological background to "an *acceptance* of guilt, a deepening of a *sense* of responsibility and a *posture* of repentance. This by no means resulted in passivity or inertness and certainly not acquiescence. On the other hand, neither did it engender a strong drive for active, practical political engagement directed toward achieving clear-cut goals."[16] Perhaps a

14. Williams, p. 115.

15. Larry L. Rasmussen, *Dietrich Bonhoeffer: Reality and Resistance* (Nashville and New York: Abingdon, 1972), p. 211.

16. Rasmussen, p. 193.

willingness to believe that words served purposes beyond and other than revealing what we are thinking would have served them well in their resistance to evil. Rasmussen, in fact, concludes that when Bonhoeffer took his reckoning of what they had learned in their resistance, he was "wrong only at one point. . . . But the mistake was deadly. 'What we shall need is not geniuses, or cynics, or misanthropes, or clever tacticians, but plain, honest, straightforward men.'"[17] This is a powerful challenge to Augustine's case, and it suggests that we may need even more arguments — which, in fact, Augustine has ready at hand.

Lying may undermine human community, and it may turn us into people whose inner self has been corrupted. Still, we may sometimes feel that lying is needed in a good cause. Augustine understands that feeling and is by no means immune to it. He considers at length how human sympathy draws us toward what he calls "compensatory sins" — lesser evils done to prevent greater evils from occurring. He gives an example of a sort still used today: a seriously ill patient who may lose the will to live if told that his son has died, but who asks whether the boy is still alive (18:171). Circumstances make it impossible to say nothing. To say either "he is alive" or "I don't know" is to lie. Yet if you tell the truth, you may (unnecessarily?) endanger the man's life. "I am," Augustine writes, "moved by these arguments — more powerfully than wisely" (18:172).

Surely the compensatory lie tempts us, tugs at us powerfully. Over against that pull Augustine sets primarily two arguments, which are the third and fourth arguments I unpack here. Each is powerful. If we give in to the lure of the compensatory lie, Augustine argues, if we acknowledge that right and

17. Rasmussen, p. 211.

wrong actions are determined solely by the balance of good and evil they accomplish, others can always place us under moral obligation if they are willing to threaten a sufficiently great evil. "The result would be that whenever the enemy who had such power said: 'Unless you are wicked I shall be more wicked, or unless you commit this crime I shall commit many such crimes,' we would feel obliged to commit the crime" (9:147-48). Augustine notes that we would be less inclined to accept this kind of reasoning if the required price involved chastity (the integrity of the body) rather than truth (the integrity of speech) (19:174). And while some might wish to disagree with him also at this point, the very structure of his argument forces us to consider whether there is any evil we would not consider ourselves obligated to do simply to avoid even greater evils threatened by others.

Related to this but coming at the issue from a slightly different angle is Augustine's belief that we must learn to think of our moral responsibilities as creaturely and therefore limited. That is, we bear moral responsibility for the evils we ourselves do, not for the wrongs we might have prevented others from doing (but did not prevent, because doing so would have required us to do wrong). "No matter how great the distance between your crime and another's, your crime is yours and not the other's" (9:149-50). Clearly, this claim extends and refines the second argument I noted above — about how a willingness to do evil corrupts our character. What this argument adds is a clear sense that moral agents are not just conduits through which things — for good or ill — happen. Who we are is revealed by what we *do* more than by what we *accomplish*. Indeed, not to suppose this is to rest the quality of our character in an entirely uncertain future. When we are willing to lie in what we take to be a good cause, we can have no certainty that good will be the result, for our power to shape events is limited (3:131). To imagine otherwise would be to lose the sense of ourselves as limited creatures under the authority of the One who is the author of our being. "Therefore, let a man do what he can even for the temporal welfare of men, but, when it comes to the point where he cannot take thought for their welfare except by sinning, then let him realize that there is nothing he can do when he sees that only that is left which he cannot rightly do" (17:170). Clearly a certain image of human beings — as creatures whose being is not only constituted by their freedom to shape themselves and their world but is also limited by the author of their being — underlies this Augustinian belief that we are not responsible for all the results that flow from our decisions and choices.

Only when we believe that might we be drawn to the fifth sort of argument Augustine offers in support of a ban on lying. The continuing influence of this last argument can be seen in a passage like the following from *Veritatis Splendor:* "Even in the most difficult situations man must respect the norm of morality so that he can be obedient to God's holy commandment. . . . Certainly, maintaining a harmony between freedom and truth occasionally demands uncommon sacrifices, and must be won at a high price: it can even involve martyrdom."[18] The Priscillianists counseled lying to conceal their identity and their beliefs. "And this great evil they deem just, for they say that what is true must be kept in the heart, but that it is no sin to utter what is false with the tongue to strangers" (2:127). Were this the right way to proceed, Augustine notes, there would never be need for martyrdom. "This opinion dishonors

18. Pope John Paul II, *The Splendor of Truth* (Boston: St. Paul Books and Media, 1993), par. 102.

the holy martyrs; nay, altogether removes the possibility of holy martyrdom. For, according to the Priscillianists, the martyrs would act more justly and wisely if they did not confess to their persecutors that they were Christians" (2:128). A church that honors its martyrs could not agree. After all, Augustine reminds Consentius, many of those who had disowned Christ rather than be martyred had not in their hearts turned against him; indeed, "almost all" of them, Augustine suspects, kept "in their hearts what they believed about Him" (6:139). But this was insufficient. The moral life is not just an interior movement or belief; it must take shape in the person's deeds. Hence, the martyr bears witness — and a kind of necessary witness — to what John Paul II calls "the inviolability of the moral order," to the limits on what we should be willing to do in order to accomplish what is good and desirable.[19] A moral world that permitted lying to avoid an evil such as persecution would have no need of martyrs, but would be a less noble world as a result. And even if the stakes are often not quite this high, an ethic that makes place for martyrs shapes the way we think about all our decisions. "Although martyrdom represents the high point of the witness to moral truth, and one to which relatively few people are called, there is nonetheless a consistent witness which all Christians must daily be ready to make, even at the cost of suffering and grave sacrifice."[20]

Interestingly, however, whereas Pope John Paul II writes that "[i]n this witness to the absoluteness of the moral good *Christians are not alone*," Augustine is less sure of that.[21] A con-

---

19. Pope John Paul II, par. 92.

20. Pope John Paul II, par. 93.

21. See paragraph 94 of *The Splendor of Truth:* "In this witness to the absoluteness of the moral good *Christians are not alone:* they are supported by the moral sense present in peoples and by the great religious and sapiential tradi-

siderable part of his discussion in *Contra mendacium* is given over to examination of certain biblical stories in which characters — sometimes honored characters — lie. Among the most interesting of these is Rahab, the prostitute in Jericho who hid two Israelite spies and then lied concerning their whereabouts to the ruler of Jericho.[22] Augustine does not seek to justify her lie, though he believes that God pardoned it. Nevertheless, he seems to think that we could not have expected Rahab to know that she should refrain entirely from lying. "When Rahab did for the Israelite spies that work which was good and laudable in view of her state of life, she was not yet such that it be demanded of her: 'Let your speech be, "Yes, yes"; "No, no"' [cf. Matt. 5:37]" (16:167). Augustine's view seems to be that before the coming of Christ and the promulgation of his teaching, Rahab could not (or might not?) have known that lying is always wrong. Presumably she would have known that one should never lie "except with the intention of wanting to benefit someone and to harm no one," a principle that might well have justified her action (16:167). "But," writes Augustine, "when we [instructed by Christ] inquire whether it is the part of a good man ever to tell a lie, we are not inquiring about the man who still belongs to Egypt or to Jericho or to Babylon or even to the earthly Jerusalem that is in slavery with her children, but about the citizen of that City above" (16:167-68).

Perhaps, Augustine seems to be intimating, his strong (exceptionless) prohibition on lying could — at best — make sense only if we hear it in the context of the revelation of God

tions of East and West, from which the interior and mysterious workings of God's Spirit are not absent."

22. The story is recounted in Josh. 2. Its result, including the rescue of Rahab after the fall of Jericho and her apparent "naturalization" as an Israelite citizen, is told in Josh. 6:22ff.

in Christ. Augustine tends to put the point in terms of what one knows or (as in Rahab's case) does not know, but I think his point is best expressed in a slightly different way. To refrain even from the "compensatory lie" we must trust that God will take responsibility for the bad consequences we may not prevent (without doing wrong). Rahab might then have said, or so Augustine surmises, "I know where they are, but I fear God and will not betray them." That is, of course, to say: Rahab might have been a martyr, enabled and strengthened by trust in "the will and power of God" to care for her either in this life or in the next (17:169). But, of course, that was not her situation; she was a citizen of Jericho, not of "that City above." Perhaps, therefore, Augustine seems to be suggesting, she does quite well (indeed, "is certainly approaching justice and deserves to be praised — though not yet in reality, still, in hope and disposition") if she "never lies except with the intention of wanting to benefit someone" (16:167).

And suddenly, in the midst of this rigorist argument for an absolute ban on lying, a "gentler" Augustine emerges. Not only for those like Rahab, who are still outside the City of God, but also for its pilgrim members who day by day are being renewed after the image of Christ, a certain patience is appropriate and pardon for the compensatory lie is available (20:177-78). It is available, however, not as an excuse or as cheap grace, but as pardon for those who want to live in the One who is truth and who believe that "No lie is of the truth" (16:168). Along the way, however, these pilgrims may sometimes find themselves saying with Augustine: "[B]ecause we are men and live among men, I confess that I am not yet in the number of those who are not troubled by compensatory sins. Often, in human affairs, human sympathy overcomes me and I am unable to resist" (18:171).

Complicating Augustine's Account

Augustine helps us to see how inadequate are views that would set aside duty simply to achieve good results. Nevertheless, we might still wonder whether there are not circumstances in which lying (not just deception or keeping silent) is in fact both permitted and right. We might, that is, wonder whether there are not some exceptions that ought to be written into Augustine's ban on lying. If these exceptions are not derived simply by an appeal to good consequences, on what are they based? Sometimes, I think, they may grow out of our sense that Augustine's vision of the uses of language is too circumscribed and that words may at times rightly be weapons. And sometimes it may be that a kind of mutual agreement exists among us that lying is permitted or even desirable in certain situations. We can examine each of these possibilities in turn.

We noted earlier how Augustine makes a sharp distinction between (permitted) deception and (forbidden) lying. But one can do this only, I think, by holding a very restricted view of the purpose of human language — as, in fact, Augustine may have. In his view words seem to have one use only. "Augustine was convinced that human speech existed for the sole purpose of communication of thought."[23] Words are "instruments to be used 'so that each person may transfer his thoughts *(cogitationes)* to the understanding *(notitiam)* of another.'"[24] This overlooks, however, many other important uses of words

23. Thomas Feehan, "The Morality of Lying in St. Augustine," *Augustinian Studies* 21 (1990): 71. See also Augustine's own statement in *Faith, Hope, and Charity* (7:32): "Surely, language was appointed not that by it men should deceive each other, but that through its instrumentality one man might make known his thoughts to another."

24. Griffiths, p. 93.

— to weave a spell, to soothe or excite, to reassure, and (importantly for our purposes) to attack or defend.

Many of the exceptional cases taken up in discussions of lying involve one or another version of an "assailant at the door" searching for someone who is hidden. Augustine himself discusses such situations — and, in fact, the case of Rahab is an excellent example. If it is right to lie to the would-be evildoer in such circumstances, as I think it is, that is not because, having compared the likely outcomes of different possible courses of action, we conclude that lying would accomplish the most good on the whole. It is not approving doing evil in order to achieve good. On the contrary, lying is here the right thing to do. It is an exception — which will apply to all cases that are similar in the relevant respects — to the rule that prohibits lying. Justifying lying here is not unlike justifying the use of force to intervene against one threatening to harm an innocent person. The difference is that, in the case of lying, words are our weapon. In both instances, though, what we do is a work of love protecting the innocent against a would-be evildoer.

Striking as these sorts of cases are (especially when we encounter them in a thinker such as Augustine or Kant, each of whom holds that even in these circumstances it would be wrong to lie), there are, I think, more poignant, and perhaps even more persuasive, instances in which lying in response to an unjust demand seems right. Bonhoeffer has offered one for us to consider:

> [A] teacher asks a child in front of the class whether it is true that his father often comes home drunk. It is true, but the child denies it. The teacher's question has placed him in a situation for which he is not yet prepared. He feels only that what is taking place is an unjustified interference

in the order of the family and that he must oppose it. What goes on in the family is not for the ears of the class in school. . . . As a simple no to the teacher's question the child's answer is certainly untrue; yet at the same time it nevertheless gives expression to the truth that the family is an institution *sui generis* and that the teacher had no right to interfere in it. The child's answer can indeed be called a lie; yet this lie contains more truth, that is to say, it is more in accordance with reality than would have been the case if the child had betrayed his father's weakness in front of the class. According to the measure of his knowledge, the child acted correctly. The blame for the lie falls back entirely upon the teacher.[25]

Which of us is not on this child's side? The teacher's unjust demand, forgetting or ignoring the truth that "not everyone has a right to know everything," should be resisted.[26] The weapon of choice for that justified resistance is words, lying words, and the child acts rightly in resisting.

There are other moments in life, though, when the apparent need to lie grows less out of the need to resist an unjust demand than out of a kind of mutual agreement that in certain situations lying is justified. Here again there are dramatic cases — espionage, for example. Nation-states have a shared (if generally tacit) understanding that deception and falsehood will be part of their mutual stock-in-trade. For anyone who thinks in the categories of Christian theology, of course, this fact will ultimately bear witness to a world that has been disordered by sin — a world that is, as Helmut Thielicke liked to

---

25. Dietrich Bonhoeffer, *Ethics* (New York: Macmillan, 1955), pp. 367-68.
26. Williams, p. 117.

put it, "the objectification of my own Babylonian heart."[27] But then the very existence of government, God's good servant for our good, bears witness to this same disorder. We can recognize the disorder without thinking ourselves guilty for existing within it. Sometimes, as in Bonhoeffer's "reckoning" for his fellow conspirators, we may feel ourselves so trapped and embedded within it that we are tempted to suppose that whatever we do is sin — and then, as in Le Carré's story, the spy may finally want to come in from the cold. Understandable — indeed, profound — as that is, I am still inclined to say with Bernard Williams that "if it is right to lie, in this kind of case it is no sign of a good disposition to feel bad about it."[28]

Here again, however, I think the more interesting and instructive cases occur when — at least in geopolitical terms — the stakes are far lower. An example from "Miss Manners" is to the point. Discussing how complex the concept of telling "the truth" is, she writes:

It means getting to the truth of the situation, rather than crude literal surface truth. To answer the question, "Would you like to see some pictures of my grandchildren?" with the directly literal truth, "No! Anything but that!" would be cruel. But is that the real question? The real question, if one has any sensitivity to humanity, is, "Would you be kind enough to let me share some of my sentiments and reassure me that they are important and worthwhile?" to which a decent person can only answer, "I'd love to."[29]

27. Helmut Thielicke, *Theological Ethics*, vol. 1, *Foundations* (Philadelphia: Fortress, 1966), p. xxi.
28. Williams, p. 115.
29. *Cleveland Plain Dealer*, June 21, 1984, p. 5E.

We are, I suspect, confident that we want to approve the answer Miss Manners recommends — so confident that we're likely to be unsure whether we really want to call it lying. Paul Griffiths had, we recall, characterized Augustine's definition of lying as involving a "mismatch" between what is in one's heart and the words one speaks. What this example illustrates is how hard it may be to say whether such a mismatch has really occurred. Several impulses are in the heart simultaneously, and not all of them can come to expression. But if Miss Manners has recommended lying here, it would be a justified lie and one about whose value and praiseworthiness we have mutual agreement. As Bonhoeffer notes, to feel compelled — or even to pride oneself in — speaking "the truth" to every person in every situation displays a cynicism that is destructive. "Exposure is cynical; and even if the cynic . . . sets himself up to be a fanatical devotee of truth, he nevertheless fails to achieve the truth which is of decisive importance, namely, the truth that since the Fall there has been a need also for concealment."[30]

Augustine's position needs complicating in yet a third way, which also rests, I think, on our shared understanding about the way in which language that speaks truth but does not display respect for the other person cannot be praised. As I noted earlier, in his discussion of compensatory sins Augustine mentions exactly the sort of medical case that has continued to get attention up to our own time — a case in which, for example, telling a critically ill man that his son has died might undermine his strength and sap his will to live (18:171). There's much to be said for Augustine's disapproval of a lie in that situation, and, surely, it is often our inability to deal with our own mortality that inclines us to lie.

30. Bonhoeffer, *Ethics*, p. 372.

There are circumstances, however, in which direct communication is not really possible — not possible because it will not in fact communicate. Tolstoy's Ivan Ilyich knows by iron laws of logic that if all men are mortal and Caius is a man, then Caius must be mortal. But when he slots his own name into that syllogism, he cannot fully grasp its truth. Only slowly and gradually can he come to understand that he is a dying man. So, for example, discussing the way in which physicians cannot immediately communicate certain truths, Thielicke writes: "Wisdom is not something that can be imparted at any moment, like the Pythagorean theorem. It has its own time, its own hour and moment."[31] Thus, whereas Augustine thinks — on the whole, rightly — that it is the liar who thinks of words as his possession to do with as he pleases, there could also be moments when we would be mistaken to suppose that the truth is at our disposal and can be communicated simply by speaking truthfully. Coming to terms with one's death, for example, or coming to know oneself as a sexual being are truths that must, as Thielicke notes, "ripen" over time; they are not accessible at any and every moment. How, then, do we decide whether we have lied when we use speech to withhold information, or to shade or deny the truth when the hearer is not yet prepared for direct communication? "It depends," Thielicke writes of the physician, "on whether he regards his first momentary denial as the initial or preliminary stage of that process which ultimately leads to the truth, a process into and through which he is determined to lead his patient, *or* whether the denial is final, made with the intention of 'sparing' the patient to the very end any certainty as to his condition."[32] This

---

31. Thielicke, p. 560.
32. Thielicke, p. 562. It might be possible to argue that Augustine could

kind of indirect communication is easily abused, and as I noted, we are readily drawn to it by our own weakness and frailty. Moreover, in our time it has often been dismissed as an illegitimate paternalism that overrides the right of autonomous patients to know everything there is to know about their condition. Granting that such criticism is often very much to the point, it is nevertheless also true that there can be a kind of cynicism that takes refuge in such claims about autonomy and bypasses the more difficult — and humanly essential — indirect communication that bears witness to the deepest truth of our human condition.

Duty and Desire

Even if — not simply repeating Augustine but thinking along with him — we complicate his discussion and build into his prohibition of lying exceptions such as those discussed above, we are left with a duty so stringent that it must cut very deeply into our character, as deeply as does the desire for happiness. And we must wonder, then, about the relationship between duty and desire in the Christian life. This tension between what Henry Sidgwick called the "attractive" and the "imperative" ways of depicting the center of the moral life has been present for centuries in our tradition — perhaps always, but at least since Christian thought, knowing God as giver of the moral law set the ideal of the "imperative" over against the

---

make his peace with this third exception. Christopher Levenick suggests, for example, that Augustine distinguishes joking from lying in large part by concerning himself with "ultimate purposes." That is, the liar's "sole aim is deception," whereas the jester does not intend the deception to be permanent and final (p. 310).

classical emphasis upon the "attractive."[33] Augustine, of course, is heir to both emphases, as becomes evident when we set the story of the restless heart told in the *Confessions* alongside the prohibition of lying in *Contra mendacium.*

The obvious way to come to terms with this tension between the attractive and the imperative is to remember that only the pure in heart will see God — not because they have deserved it, but because only such a heart would want to rest in God. Augustine does believe this. He writes, for example, in *De mendacio* that "since every man withdraws from eternity in so far as he withdraws from truth, it is most absurd to say that by so withdrawing [from truth] one is able to arrive at any good" (7:68). More powerful, and more closely connected with the theme of the restless heart, is his explanation (in *Contra mendacium*) for why, though he is drawn by the lure of "compensatory lies," he is not persuaded by their advocates: "[W]hen I put before my mind's eye the intellectual beauty of Him from whose mouth nothing false proceeded, . . . I am so inflamed by love of such great beauty that I despise all human considerations that call me back from there" (18:172). Acknowledgment and fulfillment of our duties is not a condition for resting in God; it is a description of the only sort of person who would really want to be with God.

Holding together the attractive and the imperative in this way has the added benefit of helping to make greater sense of our duties, especially those as stringent as Augustine's prohibition of lying. In *After Virtue* Alasdair MacIntyre suggests that a rational justification of our moral principles would take the form of a threefold scheme — which we might think of as the

---

33. Henry Sidgwick, *The Methods of Ethics,* 7th ed. (1907; Indianapolis and Cambridge: Hackett, 1981), p. 105.

descriptive, the attractive, and the imperative. This scheme would include a description of our human nature as it is in its "untutored" state and an image of the good that attracts us (what we would be if our nature were perfected). The imperative then fills the gap that separates the description from the image. "The precepts which enjoin the various virtues and prohibit the vices which are their counterparts instruct us how to move from potentiality to act, how to realise our true nature and to reach our true end."[34] That is to say, our duties are intelligible. They describe the transformation that takes place when one who has been turning away from the good begins to turn toward it.

Augustine's understanding of the ban on lying provides a nice illustration of this. He is moved to reject even the tempting compensatory lie when he calls to mind the "beauty of Him from whose mouth nothing false proceeded." Speech is not simply our possession; it is God's gift to us. To recognize and acknowledge this gift in truthful words is to offer grateful praise to the One from whom it comes. Paul Griffiths makes just this point in characterizing Augustine's reason for rejecting all lies. "Lying speech is owned, controlled, taken charge of, characteristically and idiosyncratically yours. True speech is disowned, relinquished, returned as gift to its giver, definitively and universally not yours. . . . The true antonym of *mendacium,* for Augustine, is *adoratio,* or its close cousin, *confessio;* and the fundamental reason for banning the lie without exception is that when we speak duplicitously, we exclude the possibility of adoration."[35] This makes clear the connection

34. Alasdair MacIntyre, *After Virtue* (Notre Dame, Ind.: University of Notre Dame Press, 1981), p. 50.
35. Griffiths, p. 85. I, of course, have argued that some exceptions should be written into Augustine's prohibition.

Augustine discerns between the attractive and the imperative, between the telos of a human life and our moral obligations. Only as I acknowledge my words as the gift of a truthful God will I desire to praise him in words that are likewise truthful. The gap between the person I am, who is often drawn to regard words as his possession, and the person I desire to be, who can return the gift of speech to its Giver, is filled by the imperative, the prohibition of lying.

As instructive as MacIntyre's threefold scheme is, and as appealing for making sense of our duties, it may not do full justice to our experience of duty as (at least sometimes) unrewarding. As MacIntyre himself once wrote in a different context, "any account of morality which does not allow for the fact that my death may be required of me at any moment is thereby an inadequate account."[36] Put more theologically, the very possibility of martyrdom reopens the chasm between the imperative and the attractive. The existence of the church's martyrs teaches Augustine that we are sometimes obligated to relinquish certain goods, even that of life, rather than violate our duty. It suggests the possibility of an obligation that does not seem to lead to any fulfillment.

Acknowledging the possibility that martyrdom may be required and honoring the church's martyrs forces us, therefore, to complicate MacIntyre's claim that our moral duties make sense only if they are understood to specify the way to move from "untutored-human-nature-as-it-is" to "man-as-he-could-be-if-he-realised-his-*telos*."[37] On his account many of our du-

---

36. Alasdair MacIntyre, "Can Medicine Dispense with a Theological Perspective on Human Nature?" in *Knowledge, Value, and Belief,* ed. Tristram Engelhardt, Jr., and Daniel Callahan (Hastings-on-Hudson: Institute of Society, Ethics, and the Life Sciences, 1977), pp. 26-27.

37. MacIntyre, *After Virtue,* p. 52.

ties have taken on the character of "survivals," whose intelligibility cannot be explained, because early modern thinkers lost the sense of a good that, if realized, would fulfill our human nature. But thinking with Augustine about the prohibition of lying and the place of martyrdom within the moral life as he envisions it compels us to realize that — in any place and in any historical moment — duty might take on an unconditional character with no apparent connection to fulfillment of our desire for happiness. The seeming unintelligibility of our moral obligations is a permanent possibility.

If we were Stoics, who desired nothing other than to act in accord with our duty, this might not be the case. But if we think as Augustine does, if we long to rest in God — and if action in accord with duty seems to lead only to death — the gap between desire and duty remains open. Acting as duty requires will not seem to be the "way" to happiness; on the contrary, it is a way that seems to arrive at a dead end — and yet is required. Hence, the "imperative" does not chart out a path that necessarily leads from our current condition (the "descriptive") to a fulfillment we desire (the "attractive"). By making duty absolute, Augustine diverts us from our search for ways to unify (by our own power) the right and the good in life. The path from where we are to where we long to be can only be traversed and believed, but not always seen.

Thinking with Augustine about the relation between desire and duty presses us inexorably, therefore, toward a life that must be characterized by hope (not in our own power to traverse this way, but in the gracious power of God). Just as Augustine sees that trust and hope are required to do what is right even when it seems unlikely to lead to the best results on the whole, so hope is needed if we are to believe that the path of duty will lead not to a dead end but to the fulfillment of our desire to be with God. And the virtue of hope is always something more than mere "anticipation" or "expectation," terms that carry a far greater sense of certainty than does "hope." "It is," as Augustine says in his *Confessions*, "one thing to see from a mountaintop in the forests the land of peace in the distance, . . . and it is another thing to hold on to the way that leads there" (7.21). That haunting refrain of book 10 — "give what you command, and command what you will" — gives voice to a way of life for which the duties God commands may not always make sense or seem to lead to that land of peace in the distance. The gap that sometimes separates desire and duty in our lives cannot be solved by moral theory. That gap is, finally, the tension between the God who calls us to himself and the God who commands us to obey. Only the God who gives what he commands, in whom we are to hope, can overcome it.

POLITICS

D ESIRE, DUTY — and, now, politics. We look to politics for
the satisfaction of so many of our desires; yet, thinking
with Augustine should remind us that the deepest longings of
the restless human heart can never be stilled by any good that
politics provides. And because this is true, because even our
most powerful institutions cannot redeem the brokenness of
human life, we would be foolish to set aside the claims of duty in
vain attempts to produce the good results we desire. Here again,
thinking with Augustine can prove instructive and fruitful.

In John Rawls's last major work, *The Law of Peoples,* which
extends his political analysis from single democratic nations to
the international society of peoples whose political lives are or-
ganized in many different ways (and which may be "decent"
even if they are not liberal democracies), he expresses a hope
that the mere possibility of a just society of peoples may be sufficient to reconcile us to the harsh reality of social life as we often experience it. "If a reasonably just Society of Peoples
whose members subordinate their power to reasonable aims is
not possible, and human beings are largely amoral, if not in-
curably cynical and self-centered, one might ask, with Kant,

whether it is worthwhile for human beings to live on the earth."[1]

The pathos of this sentence is palpable — setting, as it does, his hopes over against the realities he discerns. Rawls acknowledges that a politics from which all "comprehensive doctrines of truth" (as he calls them) are excluded will fall short of all we desire. Because that gap is deep and wide, the very best society of peoples we might manage to build is still likely to produce many people "distraught by spiritual emptiness" (p. 127). This touch of realism is not a weakness but a strength of Rawls's view. He realizes that the political realm is neither redemptive nor salvific, and that good politics must prescind from any attempt to satisfy the longing of the restless heart.

How difficult such a politics may be, however, is apparent from the manner in which Rawls himself strains against its incompleteness. He cannot simply allow the tension between the political (with its limited commitments) and the social (with its rich array of loyalties) to stand unresolved. Political liberalism "does not regard the political and the nonpolitical domains as two separate, disconnected spaces, each governed solely by its own distinct principles" (p. 160). And however strong their loyalties — as, for example, members of families or of communities of faith — adults are "citizens first" (p. 161). No "comprehensive doctrine" can be "reasonable," Rawls supposes, if it teaches that religious beliefs ("such values as salvation and eternal life — the *Visio Dei*") may ever override the "political values of a constitutional democratic society" (p. 173). That in this great theorist of liberal democracy there should be such a moment

---

1. John Rawls, *The Law of Peoples* (Cambridge, Mass., and London: Harvard University Press, 1999), p. 128. The parenthetical page references in the following text are to this work.

that — from the perspective of a religious believer or a loyal child of a family — may seem totalitarian does not strike me as at all surprising. It is hard not to hope for more from politics than it can deliver. Augustine notes that even the best and most honest of Roman historians praised Rome too highly; but how could they not, he suggests, since they had no other and better city to praise (*City of God* 3.17). If we offer our ultimate loyalty to the political community and its goods, we suppress the desire for God that marks the deepest reaches of our humanity.

Not only desire but also duty is protected by a chastened, limited politics. Because we wait on God for redemption, our attempts to accomplish the good must have their limit and must be constrained by moral duty.[2] As Augustine says in the *Confessions* (7.21), it is "one thing to see from a mountaintop in the forests the land of peace in the distance" — that is, to discern the good we seek to attain. But "it is another thing to hold on to the way that leads there" — a way that waits on God to accomplish a good that, sometimes at least, we can find no morally acceptable way to achieve. Peter Brown once suggested that we should begin studying Augustine's political thought not in the seemingly obvious places but in book 10 of the *Confessions*.[3] There Augustine makes clear — or perhaps even first comes to realize — that the man who has been telling his life story does not really know himself, cannot find an angle from which to see himself whole and entire. Likewise, we are radi-

2. See, for example, John Milbank's comment (made, of course, in support of his own somewhat different reading of Augustine) that "In a way . . . Augustine gives priority to the stoic *officium*, duty, over the idea of virtue." *Theology and Social Theory* (Oxford and Cambridge, Mass.: Blackwell, 1990), p. 412.

3. Peter Brown, "Saint Augustine and Political Society," in *The City of God: A Collection of Critical Essays*, ed. Dorothy F. Donnelly (New York: Peter Lang, 1995), p. 19.

cally ignorant of what we actually accomplish in our action. "Outside the limits of the history told in the Bible we have [Augustine believes] no way of assessing the meaning of any action, event, or any person or institution, of any culture, society, or any epoch in the unfolding history of salvation."[4] How dangerous for such people to suppose that they should set aside present duty in an attempt to fashion some future good.

Bound by our duties, we always find ourselves caught between our desires and our possibilities. "If Augustine is a thorn in the side of those who would cure the universe once and for all, he similarly torments cynics who disdain any project of human community, or justice, or possibility."[5] Hence, although it might not be right to describe Augustine as having a developed "theory" of politics, as if the nature of the political were itself the focus of his thought, thinking with him about the place of politics in the grand sweep of the story he tells in *City of God* can prove extraordinarily instructive. This long book, written over many years, may not always be internally consistent. Certainly it may sometimes resist the questions we put to it, and we in turn should resist the attempt to claim it for a particular "theory" of politics. Augustine is after something larger than that — some sense of what it means for Christians to acknowledge and cherish the brilliance of this earthly life without ever forgetting that it is "the fragile brilliance of glass" (4.3), that "smoke has no weight" (5.17), and that we are on the way toward a city far greater and more worthy of praise than any of the communities to which we give our loyalty here and now.

Augustine's distinction between the two cities is not easy to

4. R. A. Markus, *Saeculum: History and Society in the Theology of St. Augustine* (Cambridge: Cambridge University Press, 1970), p. 158.

5. Jean Bethke Elshtain, *Augustine and the Limits of Politics* (Notre Dame, Ind.: University of Notre Dame Press, 1995), p. 91.

sort out in a single, coherent way. It is precisely these difficulties, however, that invite our reflection. Along the way we should keep in mind the quite different uses he makes of the story of the founding of Rome. Identifying Rome as "the capital of the earthly city," which was founded in a fratricide (when Cain killed Abel), he notes how that first beginning was reflected in Rome's founding, when Romulus slew Remus. "Both sought the glory of establishing the Roman state" (15.5). That glory could not be shared, however, and conflict was therefore inevitable — the conflict that always marks the earthly city in its utter opposition to the City of God. This use of the founding of Rome can represent for us a reading of *City of God* that identifies the earthly city with political regimes, the City of God (in its temporal life) with the church, and sets them as institutions over against each other.

But elsewhere in *City of God* Augustine appeals to the story of Rome's founding to make a different point. Romulus is said to have founded Rome as a city of refuge for criminals, and hence "the remission of sins, the promise which recruits the citizens for the Eternal Country, finds a kind of shadowy resemblance in that refuge of Romulus, where the offer of impunity for crimes of every kind collected a multitude which was to result in the foundation of the city of Rome" (5.17). The "capital of the earthly city" was also an intimation of grace, a "shadowy resemblance" of the peace offered by the City of God.[6] This use of the founding of Rome can represent for us a reading of *City of God* that sees

---

6. Hence, true though it is in many contexts, one cannot *simply* say, as F. E. Cranz does, that human society, "which includes kingship and empire, has no positive relation, in particular no relation of image, to the Christian society of heaven." See F. Edward Cranz, "*De Civitate Dei*, XV, 2, and Augustine's Idea of the Christian Society," in *Augustine: A Collection of Critical Essays,* ed. R. A. Markus (Garden City, N.Y.: Doubleday Anchor, 1972), p. 411.

all our temporal communities (whether political regimes or churches) as caught in a field of force between the two cities, identified entirely with neither, but swaying to and fro between these ultimate destinations. From each reading there is something to be learned, but we will begin with the second angle of vision, which teaches us to limit our political expectations — to be realists but not cynics. Before we are done, however, we will also need the first angle of vision, and it will force us to consider what our expectations of the church ought to be.

A Chastened Politics

In his *History of the Church from Christ to Constantine,* Eusebius includes a "festival oration" he gave at the dedication of one of the many churches built with the support of Constantine. Now, Eusebius says, we not only hear of God's wonders performed in the past, but we see God's deeds in our own time, and so the words of the psalmist (87:3) apply to the church: "Glorious things are spoken of you, O city of God."[7] Augustine, of course, will cite the same psalm verse at the outset of book 11 of *City of God,* when he begins his discussion of the origins and ends of the two cities. However, by book 11 the Augustine who in book 1 could refer a number of times to "this Christian era" is far less inclined to identify, as Eusebius seems to have, Constantine's support of the church as a fulfillment of biblical promises and a clear manifestation of the providential work of God.[8]

---

7. Eusebius, *The History of the Church from Christ to Constantine,* trans. G. A. Williamson (Baltimore: Penguin Books, 1963), 10.4.

8. See Robert A. Markus, "'Tempora Christiana' Revisited," in *Augustine*

For Eusebius the power of Rome and the faith of the church had come together for the benefit of humankind, and this coalescence could be identified as the work of God in history. When *City of God* was read in accord with that Eusebian vision, it offered a blueprint for the medieval vision of civil and ecclesiastical powers cooperating in the shaping of a Christian society (though with the unresolved question of which power was superior and which subservient to the other). The more fully Augustine develops his narrative of the two cities, however, the less satisfactory such a reading of *City of God* must seem. Before Augustine is done, the two cities have been depicted as standing in utter conflict — the one "created by self-love reaching the point of contempt for God," the other formed "by the love of God carried as far as contempt of self" (14.28).

We can examine the most basic aspects of Augustine's mature (and chastened) evaluation of the political realm if we look at it from two different angles — one focusing on his understanding of history, and the other looking directly at his (demythologizing) analysis of the political.

"As for this mortal life, which ends after a few days' course, what does it matter under whose rule a man lives, being so soon to die, provided that the rulers do not force him to impious and wicked acts?" (5.17).[9] This may be Augustine at his

---

and His Critics, ed. Robert Dodaro and George Lawless (London and New York: Routledge, 2000), pp. 205-6: "[T]he 'mood of heady optimism' came to a climax in the years immediately following 399, lasting to about 404, and trailed away from about 405. . . . The christianisation of the empire came to seem starkly ambiguous."

9. Even here, it is worth flagging the "provided that" proviso at the end of the sentence. Moral duty again has a kind of priority over the ends we seek to achieve, and in addition, a political regime that does not try to compel such "impious and wicked acts" is certainly better than one that does (however minor the key in which Augustine makes the assertion here).

most characteristic, hoping for very little from history. Hence, it cannot be entirely mistaken to say that for Augustine, "[a]s far as it is a matter of bettering human life in this world, of providing for greater glory, greater comfort, or greater freedom, historical changes count for nothing. . . . For people who understand the true value of things there are no final aims of a political nature."[10] As we will come to see, such an assessment needs careful qualification. In particular, to say that politics cannot serve "final" aims is not at all the same as saying that politics can never better earthly life or that historical change counts for nothing. Nonetheless, this assessment does capture something very important in Augustine's analysis of the course of history.

Augustine knew more than one sort of Christian who believed we can discern the plan of God at work in history. Eusebian triumphalism, which thought it could see God's purposes at work in the establishment of Christian empire, was only one attempt to discern the signs of the times. There were also others. Especially after the fall of Rome with its enormous symbolic significance, Christian apocalyptic speculation — which might well see in Rome's fall one of the cataclysmic events preceding the return of Christ — returned regularly to millenarianism based on the twentieth chapter of the book of Revelation. Christians eager to decipher the timetable for Christ's return, which would, they thought, mark the beginning of the church's 1,000-year reign on earth with Christ, were well known to Augustine. Indeed, as he straightforwardly puts

10. Rüdiger Bittner, "Augustine's Philosophy of History," in *The Augustinian Tradition*, ed. Gareth B. Matthews (Berkeley, Los Angeles, and London: University of California Press, 1999), pp. 353-54. Cf. Brown, "Augustine and Political Society," p. 25: "There are no verbs of historical movement in the *City of God*, no sense of progress to aims that may be achieved in history."

it, "I also entertained this notion at one time" (20.7). No longer, however. Instead, in book 20 of *City of God* Augustine fashions a new way — which was to have a very wide and long influence — of reading the last book of the Bible. For Augustine the Apocalypse does not detail a series of events that we should expect before Christ returns to reign for 1,000 years with his saints. On the contrary, the period of 1,000 years — the millennium — is "the period beginning with Christ's first coming" (20.9) and extending to the end of history and the last judgment (or perhaps till that short period before the end when the devil is loosed). Thus, we live right now in the millennium. And all the end-time events of which Revelation 20 speaks are not to be awaited as if we could chart them on a timetable that would give us a clue to God's purposes in history. Augustine draws those events back into the present; they describe in symbolic manner the current experience of the church.

In so doing, Augustine flattens out the history of the world — or at least our ability to discern the contours of its history — in the stretch of time from the first to the final coming of Christ. This is a time for faithfulness, not for expecting any decisively new action of God. What God has done decisively in Jesus we know because we have been told. What God may now be doing we do not know, because we have not been told. Thus, over against either a Eusebian attachment to Christian empire as God's work or a millenarian attempt to chart God's plan within history, Augustine's mature thought displays "a thorough-going historical agnosticism" for which, therefore, "history cannot serve as the prime medium of salvation."[11]

---

11. Paula Fredriksen, "Tyconius and Augustine on the Apocalypse," in *The Apocalypse in the Middle Ages*, ed. Richard K. Emmerson and Bernard McGinn (Ithaca, N.Y.: Cornell University Press, 1992), pp. 33-34.

Depicting the millennium as a (flattened) period of time stretching out to the end of history as we know it, Augustine has given us a reading of history not unlike his picture of the self in book 10 of the *Confessions*. A reader of the *Confessions* supposes, not unreasonably, that Augustine is telling the story of his life, narrating who he is. But those readers who progress beyond book 8 may be surprised to find that this can't be done. We cannot really know ourselves, Augustine concludes. Only God can manage that — only God can catch the human heart, see it whole, and hold it still. Hence, only God can discern the ultimate significance of any moment in a person's life. What Augustine does there for the interior history of a person, he does in book 20 of *City of God* for the external history of the world. Knowing what God has done in Christ, we can trust that history will be, finally, a story of God's triumph. But we know little about the meaning of events in the time after Christ. Just as we must be largely agnostic about the meaning of our own life, so also must we be about the course of history. From the resurrection of Christ to the end of history, nothing newly redemptive should be anticipated. Certainly we cannot and should not try to calculate where history is going, as if we could clearly identify its decisive moments or know for certain how our actions helped to produce results at which God's providence aims.

It has not been uncommon for history to be divided into periods or stages — quite often into three stages, the last of which will bring its course of development to perfection. Thus, the humanists in the Renaissance (impressed most with their own moment in time) divided history into ancient, medieval, and modern. In the eighteenth century Comte identified a theological, a metaphysical, and a (culminating) scientific period of history. Marx famously depicted movement from a phase of primitive communism, through the bourgeois class society, to (after the revolution) a classless society. And in the twentieth century there was a threefold division that had an unmistakably millenarian ring to it — from the Holy Roman Empire, to the period of Bismarck's rule, to the Third Reich, which was, in fact, to last for a thousand years. In their different ways all these thinkers believed that something decisively new was happening or was about to happen — bringing in a new age of fulfillment in which (at least on some readings) division and alienation would be no more. Augustine's interpretation of the millennium — and what it implies for our (in)ability to discern the contours of God's work in history — gives the back of the hand to all such pretensions. No earthly perfection is possible. What God is accomplishing in that period stretching from the time of Christ to the final judgment is largely hidden from us.

Our task, then, is less to look for the signs of the times than to be patient, to wait for God — and, along the way, to carry out our duties faithfully. For until God once again acts in a new and decisive way to bring history to its culmination, there is really only one thing to say about the shape of earthly life: two loves struggle within the self, two cities struggle on the world stage. Until the end of history we are caught in the midst of that struggle, and the communities to which we belong are caught in the field of force between two ultimate possibilities: the *civitas terrena* and the *civitas Dei*. At whatever moment along the way we find ourselves, even if it seems to be (and perhaps is) a moment of great progress, it is also another moment in which the struggle between the two cities continues in human history. We know the outcome of that struggle, but we have little idea of the significance of the present moment or of our place in the scheme of divine providence.

City of God does more than puncture the balloon of Christian hopes — whether Eusebian or millenarian — for a culminating and fulfilling historical moment. There is a second angle, a normative argument going well beyond historical agnosticism, from which Augustine can be seen to diminish or desacralize the significance of the political. Peter Brown writes that when Augustine opens book 19 of *City of God* by outlining the 288 theories of the good life enumerated by Marcus Varro and rejecting them all, this "marks the end of classical thought."[12] At the very least, it is clear that Augustine's well-known analysis of Cicero's definition of a res publica departs decisively from the classical vision of politics, of political community as the place where human beings are perfected in virtue.

In an essay written half a century ago, Edward R. Hardy, Jr., invited his readers to consider what Augustine would have assumed had he chanced to hear a group of contemporary American Christians singing:

> O beautiful for patriot dream
> That sees beyond the years
> Thine alabaster cities gleam
> Undimmed by human tears.

Augustine could only have assumed, Hardy suggests, that they were singing of "our true fatherland, the heavenly city which can be reached only after the sin and sorrow of this earthly pilgrimage are ended."[13] In truth, of course, these words, drawn

12. Brown, "Augustine and Political Society," p. 26.
13. Edward R. Hardy, Jr., "The City of God," in *A Companion to the Study of St. Augustine*, ed. Roy W. Battennhouse (New York: Oxford University Press, 1955), p. 258.

from the book of Revelation, would have for many of our contemporaries no referent other than or beyond "America the
Beautiful." Sincere and devoted patriotism is not a bad thing,
but, as we noted above, those who have no other and better city
to praise must inevitably make too much of the political communities they inhabit. It is the glory of politics that it may invite from us great sacrifice, even what we are often pleased
(though mistaken) to call "the ultimate sacrifice" — and it is
the terror of politics that political loyalty may so easily be un-
chastened by the danger of idolatry. Augustine offers his readers a better and more alluring city to love, and thereby he aims
to chasten the claims of politics.

Early in *City of God,* as he launches his rebuttal of pagan ob-
jections to Christianity on political grounds, Augustine mentions (without analyzing in detail) Cicero's opinion of the Roman commonwealth. And he notes that for Cicero a "people"
is characterized not as any random assembly but as an association "united by a common sense of right and a community of
interest" (2.21). Rather startlingly, Augustine claims that if one
uses this characterization, Rome never was a commonwealth.
"But, God willing, we will look into this later." And long after
his readers might have forgotten that promissory note, Augustine opens 19.21 with the words: "This brings me to the place
where I must fulfil . . . the promise I gave in the second book."

Augustine's reasoning is straightforward, even if likely at
first glance to strike us as strained. Cicero's definition of a people requires a shared sense of what is right, a shared sense of
justice. Without that, we have not a people but a random assembly. But, Augustine asks, turning the screws just a bit,
what possible justice can there be in a people among whom
God is not given his due and loved above all else? If justice is,
in the simplest sense, giving each his due, and if the true God

is not rightly honored and worshiped as is his due, then justice is not present among a people.

This argument is, I suggested, likely at first to strike us as strained — a bit too cute. Augustine seems to be saying, "Those Romans got almost everything right, but they missed this one thing. They didn't worship the true God. And so Rome never had any justice and never was a true common-wealth at all." Stated that way, the argument is unlikely to per-suade us. But that is not Augustine's argument. He is not sug-gesting that the Romans had most things right and simply overlooked one important matter. He is claiming that to miss this one thing, to get it wrong and not to worship the true God, is bound to disorder the whole of life. Everything else will be distorted and tainted, loved in a way that is not quite right — since, after all, nothing can be seen and loved for what it really is unless seen in relation to God. Hence, where God is not given his due, any order we create will be some form of disor-der. Any justice we attain will be some species of injustice. The relation to God affects everything else. It reaches down into ev-ery aspect of life — including the political — to give shape and form. Hence, if God is not rightly honored, true justice cannot possibly be present, and in accord with Cicero's own character-ization, there cannot be a people in the strict sense. How could it be otherwise unless we have another and better city to praise?

In demythologizing or desacralizing the political, Augus-tine does indeed depart from the classical characterization of the city as the final and self-sufficient community — the place where individuals fully develop their humanity and come to flourish. In its place Augustine offers his own definition of a people, and it is a characterization from which much of the high moral purpose — and any hint of ultimacy — has been effectively drained. A people is simply an "association of . . . rational beings united by a common agreement on the objects of their love" (19.24). Judging from this angle, Augustine has no difficulty affirming that "the Roman people is a people" (19.24) — better at some times than at others, to be sure, depending on the loves that bind it together.

If political communities are in this way effectively desacralized, if we could never from this perspective imagine that rulers might simply be christened as agents who help to usher in God's kingdom, we must also note something else, something more positive. From this angle political communities — even if they can never constitute even a beginning of the *civitas Dei* — are also not the *civitas terrena*. Although Augustine can sometimes refer to Rome, the paradigmatic political community, as an instantiation of the earthly city (18.2), as a "second Babylon" (18.22), or as "the capital of the earthly city" (15.5), his chastened definition of political community, having eliminated ultimacy from politics, actually makes room for a somewhat more positive evaluation of Rome. As it cannot be the City of God, so also it cannot be *the* earthly city. Hence, distinctions — finely grained judgments of better or worse — are possible. Augustine leaves no doubt that ancient republican Rome was, in his mind, far better than the empire of his own day. He cannot entirely withhold his admiration from those ancient Romans who sought "glory in their country's safety above their own and . . . suppressed greed for money and many other faults in favour of that one fault of theirs, the love of praise." If we should not finally call them good or righteous in the full sense, we can nonetheless say: "If men have not learnt to restrain their discreditable passions by obtaining the help of the Holy Spirit . . . , at least it is good that the desire for human praise and glory makes them, not indeed saints, but less depraved men" (5.13). This is the angle of vision from which one might discern in Rome's founding as a city of refuge a "shadowy resemblance" of the forgiveness of sins (5.17) — a striking thing indeed to say of "the capital of the earthly city."

This is also the angle from which a certain understanding of the "two cities," an understanding developed most influentially by R. A. Markus, naturally emerges.[14] Its contours are apparent already in 1.35, where Augustine characterizes the two cities as "interwoven and intermixed in this era," awaiting "separation at the last judgment." Some who seem to be enemies of the City of God will in the end be seen as her citizens. Others whose membership in the heavenly city seems evident to us "will not join with her in the eternal destiny of the saints" (1.35). From this angle it would be difficult to identify either of the cities with any empirical institution (such as "state" or "church"). The cities are eschatological realities, available for our examination only at the end of time. Only God knows the secret of their membership, and only God could therefore locate them within our history. As eschatological realities they are utter opposites. Tracing the origin of the two cities back to Cain and Abel, Augustine notes that "the conflict between Cain and Abel displayed the hostility between the two cities themselves" (15.5).

This is a profound, even moving, theological analysis of human history, but, we might wonder, what possible political good could it be to us? What good is it to speak of these two cities if we can never point to, locate, or identify them? The answer, I think, is that even though on this reading the two cities have no identifiable location, they provide a set of lenses

14. Markus, *Saeculum*.

through which to view the actual, empirically available, communities within which we live. We should anticipate and expect that in the institutions of any society the two cities — formed by their contrasting loves — will be inextricably intermingled. That anticipation may in fact help us achieve a certain political wisdom.

Perhaps the most important lesson this analysis can teach us is that our actual communities — which are simply a swaying to and fro between these two ultimate possibilities — will always be characterized by division and friction. The conflict between the two cities (symbolized by Cain's killing of Abel) means that the life of any community must be disordered — and, hence, that life will be marked not only by the eschatological conflict between the City of God and the earthly city but also by division and conflict within society (symbolized by the killing of Remus by Romulus). Therefore: no return to paradise. No utopia. No end to friction and strife. No tone of surprise or outrage when politics turns out to be more complicated and less amenable to our ideals than we had imagined. The best we can hope for, and a mark of political wisdom, is that our divisions and disagreements be channeled and controlled in creative and fruitful ways.

Division and conflict need not mean sheer chaos, however. Any city, if it is to be a city at all, will fashion some sort of peace. It will be a brittle peace, founded on fear and force. War may need to be waged in service of this peace (19.12). Even so, a peace that is not entirely just remains "so great a good that . . . no word ever falls more gratefully upon the ear, nothing is desired with greater longing" (19.11). Every actual society combines impulses toward a common good — a good that will flow back on all and that no one need fear to share — with impulses toward pursuit of private, competitive interests. (Hence, Rome is both founded on a fratricide *and* offers in its founding an intimation of grace.) Madison's famous comment in number 51 of *The Federalist Papers* captures well the modest expectations we should have for politics in such a world: "Ambition must be made to counteract ambition. . . . It may be a reflection on human nature that such devices should be necessary to control the abuses of government. But what is government itself but the greatest of all reflections on human nature? If men were angels, no government would be necessary."[15]

The *civitas Dei* and *civitas terrena,* understood as eschatological realities, offer therefore a useful lens through which to examine the good of politics and reflect upon its limits. Looked at from this angle, the first thing Christians must say is no to political pretension. Some cities are better, others worse — but none is the City of God. We are pilgrims traveling toward another and better city that for now must remain an object of faith and hope. We may sometimes be fortunate enough to find in our historical communities intimations of that better city, but still, "smoke has no weight." Hence, Augustine teaches us to say no to the Aristotelian ideal of politics as a self-sufficient realm in which human life comes to full realization — and more generally to any totalitarian or utopian vision that might cut off the heart's longing for God. None of us belongs wholly and entirely to the realm of politics, and the desire that moves us at the deepest reaches of our being cannot be satisfied by any political good.

On this reading of the two cities, then, both Augustine's analysis of the course of history and his desacralizing of politics give us what can rightly be described as a remarkably "real-

15. Alexander Hamilton, James Madison, and John Jay, *The Federalist Papers* (New York: New American Library, 1961), p. 322.

istic" understanding of the political.[16] It has no ultimacy about it, and political rule will one day cease when citizens of the heavenly city are no longer in their present pilgrim condition. Shorn of any ultimate significance, the societies in which we live might nevertheless be useful meeting places — a kind of neutral ground — for those who, though sharing no ultimate loyalties, desire the great good of earthly peace. We might, that is, read Augustine as a proto-Rawlsian, for whom the political fashioning of peace can be successful precisely because politics is a realm denuded of religious commitments.[17] Robert Markus, on whose careful work I have drawn for this depiction of our identifiable communities as caught within a field of force between the two cities — which are themselves eschatological, not empirical, entities — makes the point in precisely that way: "The main lines of his [Augustine's] thinking about history, society and human institutions in general (the *saeculum*) point towards a political order to which we may not unreasonably apply the anachronistic epithet 'pluralist,' in that it is neutral in respect of ultimate beliefs and values."[18]

A Chastened but Not Denuded Politics

Not only does the term "pluralist" seem anachronistic when applied to Augustine, it will of course appear surprising when

16. Reinhold Niebuhr, "Augustine's Political Realism," in *The City of God: A Collection of Critical Essays*, pp. 119-34. Cf. p. 120: "Augustine was, by general consent [!], the first great 'realist' in Western history." Niebuhr also says "Augustine's realism was . . . excessive" (p. 123).

17. For one argument of this sort, see Edmund N. Santurri, "Rawlsian Liberalism, Moral Truth and Augustinian Politics," *Journal for Peace and Justice Studies* 8, no. 2 (1997): 1-36.

18. Markus, *Saeculum*, p. 151.

we consider his well-known willingness to approve — under certain circumstances and within certain limits — religious coercion by Roman imperial power in service of the church.[19] Yet, at least on the reading of *City of God* I have given thus far, the term makes some sense. In effect, Markus writes, Augustine's political vision (as it comes to fruition in book 19 of *City of God*) "pushed such fundamental commitments as a man's religious beliefs and the values he lives by outside the field of political discourse." Religious beliefs are characterized by Markus as "inward" and excluded from politics, which is confined to the "outward." The political realm, in turn, is structured around "coincident [outward] decisions" that arise from "fundamentally differing [inward] structures of motivation."[20] This is strikingly similar to Rawls's influential depiction of a liberal democracy as one having "no final ends and aims," and having as a seemingly "permanent feature" of its "public culture" a plurality of "reasonable comprehensive religious, philosophical, and moral doctrines."[21]

19. See Markus, *Saeculum*, chap. 6, and Peter Brown, "St. Augustine's Attitude to Religious Coercion," in *Religion and Society in the Age of Saint Augustine* (London: Faber and Faber, 1972), pp. 260-78. That Augustine envisioned religious coercion as a kind of pastoral discipline appropriately undertaken by Christian rulers seems to me true — and understandable, if not entirely defensible. But it is difficult to find room for such an understanding if we read the two cities simply as eschatological realities — and certainly if we take that reading to lead in turn to a depiction of the political realm as religiously denuded and inherently pluralistic.

20. Markus, *Saeculum*, p. 70. If Markus had not been writing in 1970, we might have supposed that he had in mind Rawls's concept of an "overlapping consensus."

21. John Rawls, *Political Liberalism* (New York: Columbia University Press, 1996), pp. 41, 36. Rawls also sees "unreasonable" comprehensive doctrines in a society, but they have no claim on others and cannot participate in any overlapping consensus. It may also be worth noting that Rawls did not interpret

In a final twist Rawls gave to the convoluted development of his thought, he allowed religious believers engaged in "public reasoning" to appeal to their comprehensive doctrines, but only "provided that in due course public reasons, given by a reasonable political conception, are presented sufficient to support whatever the comprehensive doctrines are introduced to support."[22] If this draws back slightly from a politics entirely denuded of religious beliefs, it should not satisfy serious religious believers — not even those drawn to a kind of Augustinian realism. And before we consider the possibility of another and different reading of the two cities, it is worth seeing that even on the reading given above — even considering the two cities as eschatological realities that cannot be identified with any empirical institutions — Augustine's understanding of politics is by no means one stripped bare of "comprehensive doctrines." The realm of politics lacks ultimacy; it is neither redemptive nor salvific. But it is by no means a realm in which religious beliefs, and visions of the moral life shaped by such beliefs, have no proper place.[23]

---

the Augustinian strain of Christian belief as affirming an inevitable and reasonable plurality of goods in politics. Cf. p. 134: "One of the deepest distinctions between conceptions of justice is between those that allow for a plurality of reasonable though opposing comprehensive doctrines each with its own conception of the good, and those that hold that there is but one such conception to be recognized by all citizens who are fully reasonable and rational. Conceptions of justice that fall on opposite sides of this divide are distinct in many fundamental ways. Plato and Aristotle, and the Christian tradition as represented by Augustine and Aquinas, fall on the side of the one reasonable and rational good. Such views hold that institutions are justifiable to the extent that they effectively promote that good."

22. Rawls, *Political Liberalism*, pp. li-lii.

23. It is worth noting that Markus was led to amend slightly the vision of politics he had at certain points characterized as Augustinian in *Saeculum* (as, for example, when he described the values people live by as "outside the

One simple reason for declining to suppose that Augustinian realism must or ought lead to a politics entirely untouched by larger comprehensive views (whether specifically religious or not) is that such a politics is a mirage and cannot be achieved. Those who profess neutrality often turn out to be intensely committed to views that rely on deeper metaphysical or normative commitments. An all-too-obvious case in point is the long footnote Rawls devotes to what he calls "the troubled question of abortion."[24] Balancing the three political values he thinks are most clearly involved (respect for human life, reproduction of a society over time, and equality of women as citizens), he quickly concludes: "Now I believe any reasonable balance of these three values will give a woman a duly qualified right to decide whether or not to end her pregnancy." Moreover, "any comprehensive doctrine that leads to a balance of political values excluding that duly qualified right in the first trimester is to that extent unreasonable." Such a view manages to be simultaneously ad hoc and

---

realm of political discourse"). Thus, for example, in a later essay Markus notes that, as *City of God* grew and developed over the years of its writing, Augustine found himself unable simply to polemicize against the Roman Empire (and the "pride" that shaped it). Without retracting that critique of Rome, Augustine reaches toward a "mature complexity" that Markus describes as "a duality: government seen as domination and government seen as guardian of the common good." Government as guardian of the common good opens up space for a politics no longer denuded of normative commitments based on beliefs about human nature. R. A. Markus, *"Di ciuitate dei:* Pride and the Common Good," in *Sacred and Secular: Studies on Augustine and Latin Christianity* (London: Variorum, 1994), III: 253. We should note, however, that at some points in *Saeculum* Markus describes an Augustine who would not have pushed "values" outside the realm of politics: "In matters falling short of the ultimate purposes society must concern itself with shaping the pattern of its common values" (p. 70).

24. Rawls, *Political Liberalism*, p. 243 n. 32. He himself returns to this footnote and tries to salvage it in yet another footnote on p. 169 of *The Law of Peoples*. I do not think the salvage operation succeeds.

(unwittingly) laden with normative commitments. That Rawls should so readily think contrary views unreasonable might well make us skeptical about his ability really to eschew the deeper commitments carried by comprehensive doctrines. Likewise, one need not listen long to public discussion in the United States of embryonic stem cell research to note how deeply it is shaped by commitments grounded in what Rawls would have called comprehensive doctrines. We are accustomed, of course, to saying this of those who oppose such research (based in part on beliefs about the full humanity of embryos), but it is equally true that proponents of research regularly appeal to claims (often, to be sure, largely unexamined) about the meaning of suffering and the necessity of overcoming it — to claims, that is, about "the meaning of life."

There are, however, deeper reasons for believing that an Augustinian vision of politics as nonredemptive need not be the same as a politics characterized by only the most minimal moral commitments or agreements. Augustine is not unfamiliar with a public realm from which all but the thinnest of moral agreements are absent. Indeed, consider his satirical depiction (which has an amazingly contemporary ring) of the kind of happiness desired by lovers of the pagan gods: "The laws should punish offences against another's property, not offences against a man's own personal character. No one should be brought to trial except for an offence, or threat of offence, against another's property, house, or person; but anyone should be free to do as he likes about his own, or with his own, or with others, if they consent" (2.20).

What Augustine here satirizes, contemporary American culture often regards as desirable. Thus, for example, in the spring of 2004 the U.S. Supreme Court ruled (in *Ashcroft v. ACLU*) that legislation known as the Child Online Protection Act, designed to protect children from Internet pornography, was in probable violation of the free speech guarantees of the First Amendment to the Constitution. This ruling should have been no surprise to those who have paid attention to the Court's difficulties in finding any claims more overriding than those of choice and consent. In 1992, in *Planned Parenthood v. Casey,* the last major abortion decision handed down by the Court, Justice Kennedy wrote: "At the heart of liberty is the right to define one's own concept of existence, of meaning, of the universe, and of the mystery of human life." Likewise, in *Lawrence v. Texas* (a ruling in 2003 that invalidated an antisodomy law in Texas) Justice Kennedy (again) wrote that the several states may not "define the meaning of the 'intimate sexual' relationship or . . . set its boundaries absent injury to a person or abuse of an institution the law protects." Granting the complexities these cases and issues involve, it would be hard to deny that the kind of position displayed in them fits well the sort of public sphere Augustine described in order to satirize and reject. Moreover, we can reject such a denuded public sphere without making the kind of mistakes that Augustine's agnosticism about the course of history was intended to deflect. Caring for the common good, and recognizing that this means caring for more than mutual consent, does not mean being governed by the illusion that America (or any country) can know that it serves God's providence in some special way. Sometimes, perhaps, events will serve to remind us of this truth, when we realize how little we can understand or master the complex — indeed, well nigh inscrutable — forces at work in the geopolitical world. We should want to be better than we are, but perhaps we should not suppose that we can be what John Winthrop had in mind: a city set on a hill as an exemplar of divine purpose. That is at least part of what it means to eschew a redemptive politics — to free ourselves from the illusion that we are so certain of the purposes of providence that we can be the engine driving them in human history. But freeing ourselves of that illusion does not mean freeing ourselves of our religious beliefs whenever we step into the public sphere.

If Aristotle was at all right to suggest that ethics is a branch of politics and that a good polity must pay attention to the (moral) education of the young, government may need to guard and shape the common life of a people in ways that pay attention to what is "inward" and what motivates behavior. It cannot make choice and consent the only values it recognizes. Attempts to protect children from Internet pornography offer a clear example of the problem. True as it may be that this should be the primary responsibility of parents, they face daunting obstacles and almost inevitable failure without a supportive "moral ecology" in the surrounding society.[25] Understanding this, we can also understand why — despite all the puzzles it has created for commentators over the years — Augustine might quite naturally have approved governmental religious coercion (more reluctantly with respect to Donatists, Christian heretics, than with respect to pagans).

To understand is not of course to endorse, but we should be clear about why we do not want to follow Augustine here. Trying to explain how Augustine might have come to this point, Markus notes that Augustine thought of rulers who were Christians primarily as members of the church. Thus, even at a point where his theology had shifted in such a way that one might suppose he would have rejected governmental coercion, Augustine "continued to speak of Christian rulers and officials owing specific service to God in their public, offi-

---

25. Robert P. George, *Making Men Moral: Civil Liberties and Public Morality* (Oxford: Clarendon, 1995), p. 45.

cial capacity."[26] This does not strike me as a very helpful criticism of Augustine — as if he should have recommended, or we should recommend, deliberate compartmentalization of religious beliefs by anyone who happens to act in a public capacity. On the contrary, Christians in public service should decline to use political power to (attempt to) create faith precisely because they take seriously their religious commitments — among them the belief that God wills to work faith not through the power of the sword but through the word of the gospel and the testimony of the Holy Spirit. Augustine saw this only in part. He saw that political rule occupies a penultimate place in God's governance of history — that it is intended to end and that its chief function is to preserve the world toward the redemption God works in other ways. But he did not work out, or not fully work out, the implications of that theological vision, and it is more important for us to try to get it right than to try to make Augustine consistent.

Given those caveats, there is much to be learned from Augustine's mature thought. Thus, for example, in a long passage in *City of God* (19.17) he describes the earthly peace produced by earthly cities, a peace that Christians gratefully receive and value. This earthly peace is possible, at least in part, precisely when politics does not seek to shape shared religious belief. "So also the earthly city, whose life is not based on faith, aims at an earthly peace, and it limits the harmonious agreement of citizens concerning the giving and obeying of orders to the establishment of a kind of compromise between human wills about the things relevant to mortal life." After all, though at the end we will have membership in only one city, "this mortal condition is shared by both cities," and "a harmony may be preserved

26. Markus, *Saeculum*, p. 147.

between them in things that are relevant to this condition." Augustine does not — could not — have in mind the kind of arrangement that Americans have come to characterize in terms of "separation of church and state," but he does see that a politics from which redemptive ultimacy has been drained is a politics that is in many respects good for the church, which "could not have laws of religion [in] common with the earthly city." Hence, Christians not only acquiesce in the limitations of politics; in some respects they welcome them. "Thus even the Heavenly City in her pilgrimage here on earth makes use of the earthly peace and defends and seeks the compromise between human wills in respect of the provisions relevant to the mortal nature of man, so far as may be permitted without detriment to true religion and piety."

We should not of course confuse these limits with a concept of "separation" of church and state that drives religious language entirely out of the public realm. Some forms of "religion" in public life (even though they are seldom sufficiently religious really to satisfy believers, and may even be worrisome to them) are actually useful reminders of the limits of politics. For example, "In God we trust" on American coins, pledging allegiance to a nation characterized as "under God," a day of national thanksgiving — all are ways by which the U.S. government commits itself to "a profound self-limitation."[27] These are religious expressions but with "purely negative content."[28] They do not prescribe, much less coerce, religious belief; rather they bear witness that government "denies itself any authority to exercise jurisdiction over the sacred."[29]

27. Robert W. Tuttle, "One Nation under God?" *Cresset* 67 (April 2004): 52.

28. Tuttle, p. 53.

29. Tuttle, p. 52.

Thinking with Augustine, therefore, we might come to endorse a politics free of redemptive purpose while simultaneously distinguishing that from a politics entirely neutral with respect to competing visions of the good life or entirely deprived of religious reference in public life. The earthly peace welcomed by the heavenly city is an agreement about "the things relevant to mortal life." It is "secular" in the sense that it is confined to this age that is passing away and is not of eternal significance. Still, we might ponder what things are relevant to this temporal, mortal life with which political agreement concerns itself.[30]

Suppose my neighbor thinks spouses who grow weary of each other should be able to divorce, no questions asked, and I do not. Is this a component of the good life on which public neutrality is required or desirable? Is it a thing relevant to mortal life that may be encompassed within our political agreement? Suppose I think people seeking assistance in suicide should be permitted such help and my neighbor disagrees. Is this a matter relevant to our mortal life and, as such, a fit matter for political judgment? Or is it just an instance of different comprehensive worldviews — between which the state should be neutral? Suppose I think the retarded should be denied forms of medical care available to the rest of us, and my neighbor disagrees. All the same questions arise. And in fact, as I noted above in connection with Rawls's footnote on abortion, purported governmental neutrality on such questions involving competing visions of the good life will often amount to unacknowledged support for one of the competing perspectives.

30. In the following paragraphs I draw on my earlier essay, " 'The Things Relevant to Mortal Life': Divorcing Augustine from Rawls," *Journal for Peace and Justice Studies* 8, no. 2 (1997): 63-68.

Rawls himself, in order to argue that abolitionist and civil rights movements, which he wants to approve, did not violate the restrictions he places on public argument, is driven to suggest tortuously that these activists did not act unreasonably, "or rather, they did not provided they thought, or on reflection would have thought (as they certainly could have thought), that the comprehensive reasons they appealed to were required to give sufficient strength to the political conception to be subsequently realized."[31] If we unpack this argument, it really says the following: Religious *faith* sought *understanding* and found it in a political vision that condemned slavery and second-class citizenship. Because it was genuine understanding of the human condition that had been uncovered by religious believers, they were able to communicate that vision to others. As it gradually came to be seen as common wisdom, even those who did not share the religious vision undergirding it came to regard it as true. But if this "unpacking" of his explanation is accurate, it means that antecedent limits on the kinds of arguments admitted into public may deprive us of truths we need to see, truths that are relevant to the life we share in political community.

Recent debates about new reproductive technologies offer yet another illustration of how easily we may narrow our vision of things relevant to this mortal life. A certain form of argument has become common and is offered as a plausible way of treating such issues in a morally pluralistic society. The argument begins, as always, with autonomy. It is important, we are told, that human beings have the widest possible freedom to make their life choices. In particular, certain decisions — such as whether to have a child — are of such personal significance that they should, as much as possible, be

31. Rawls, *Political Liberalism*, p. 251.

free from constraint. Of course, this freedom is not absolute. It may have to be limited to protect others from harm. If, for example, children resulting from in vitro fertilization (IVF) were significantly more likely to be born prematurely and to suffer from such prematurity, that might be a good reason to limit the use of IVF. But no other sort of reason for limitation is acknowledged.

Some people might think IVF should be limited to married couples, because they hold that childbearing (and child rearing) is appropriate only in that setting. Some might hold that any IVF procedure using donor gametes should be prohibited, believing that such procedures blur important kinship lines or inappropriately bring third parties into a marital relation. Some might argue that surrogacy should be forbidden on the ground that it demeans women to use their person as a manufacturing site. Some might contend that people who are carriers of genetic diseases — or who desire a child of a certain sex — should not be permitted to use IVF to select certain embryos for implantation while discarding others. Some might hold that IVF technology should not be used at all, believing that such a process of "manufacture" threatens the equal dignity of the child who is produced.

We can imagine a wide variety of such views. None of them, however, is precisely about "harms" caused by IVF. Rather, each proposes — or might propose — to limit, or forbid, the use of IVF technology in some situations because it is thought to be wrong in a specifiable way. Each thinks that, at least under certain circumstances, the use of IVF demeans the dignity of human persons, or teaches us to think of the next generation in ways that do not involve unqualified acceptance, or makes more difficult the maintenance of an affective bond across the generations — and so forth. And on the basis of such "wrongs," each of these views might propose limits on re-productive freedom, limits on personal autonomy.

But the form of argument that has become common will characterize such limits as too speculative or "symbolic" to be allowed public purchase in a pluralistic society.[32] And it is true that such limits would not be entirely neutral with respect to competing visions of the good life (or the common good of a society). For such views, were they fully developed, would be grounded in an understanding of what is normatively human. They propose, at least implicitly and often explicitly, a vision of what it means for human beings to flourish.

If we suppose that the religious neutrality of a state (that is, it does not aim at the salvation of its citizens nor see itself as having any unique connection to God's redemptive purposes in history) is equivalent to neutrality with respect to competing visions of the good life, we will have to look to thinkers other than Augustine for theoretical support. A chastened, realistic, nonredemptive politics is not a politics denuded of attention to and care for a wide range of matters — the bond between the generations, the dignity of the human body, the connection be-tween marriage and procreation, the worth of weak and voice-less human beings. Such concerns are relevant to this mortal life and are simultaneously part of our comprehensive visions of the morally good life.

Thus, while Augustine desires a peaceable politics (as book 19 of *City of God* powerfully demonstrates), he does so chiefly for one reason: the peaceable state makes possible the church's mission in its present pilgrim condition. This is something

32. See, for example, John A. Robertson, *Children of Choice: Freedom and the New Reproductive Technologies* (Princeton: Princeton University Press, 1994).

other than and different from a simple desire that conflict be avoided; indeed, mere avoidance of conflict is not of overriding importance to Augustine. He understood well that conflict about things relevant to this mortal life is inevitable and not always or altogether undesirable. As Robert Merrihew Adams has noted, "in politics . . . conflict could hardly be eradicated without excluding from the political process the selfhood of most of the individuals, and the identity of many of the groups, in society."[33] By contrast, "[a] certain anxiety pervades Rawls's argument: he is unnerved by the prospect of 'uninhibited, robust, and wide-open' debate. His argument about public reason is distinguished by a kind of nervousness, manifested in public reason's desire to exclude. This fear gives rise to the attempt to fix a conception of justice, at least in broad outline, in advance, to draw limits around acceptable arguments and modes of debate, and to ensure that discussion proceeds along the proper channels."[34] Why this anxiety? Perhaps because the neutral society is the best city Rawls can imagine. Or, perhaps, because he has no other city to love. A truly chastened politics, knowing the limited time and purpose of political rule, need not be marked by such anxiety.

A Politics Limited and Protected by the Church

Clearly, then, a reading of the two cities as eschatological communities — which cannot be identified with any community

33. Robert Merrihew Adams, "Religious Ethics in a Pluralistic Society," in *Prospects for a Common Morality*, ed. Gene Outka and John P. Reeder, Jr. (Princeton: Princeton University Press, 1993), p. 106.

34. Peter C. Meilaender, "The Problem of Having Only One City: An Augustinian Response to Rawls," *Faith and Philosophy* 20 (April 2003): 182.

to which one might point, but which instead provide a perspective from which to discern the contrary pulls within all societies — offers an instructive angle from which to think as
Christians about politics. The political communities within
which we live, though certainly not to be identified with the
civitas Dei, are also not the *civitas terrena.* They exist within the
continuing tension between those contrary pulls, the tension
that constitutes the story of human history — and might be
said to be open to each of them. Marked by that duality, they
are places where, sometimes, intimations of the greater peace
of the City of God can be dimly seen (even though no way
leads from those intimations to that greater peace itself). They
are also places where God makes possible a modest sort of
peace — setting ambition over against counterambition, force
against counterforce. As we have seen, however, these limits
do not mean that religious or metaphysical beliefs have no
place in a chastened politics. Incapable of satisfying the deepest desire of the human heart, the state ought never claim our
ultimate loyalty; yet, it is not and cannot be "neutral" with respect to all conceptions of the good life.

Instructive as this reading may be when we think about politics, true to what Augustine says in many places as it is, it nevertheless falls short in one crucial respect. It cannot do justice to
the nature and presence of the church within human history.
According to this first way of interpreting the meaning of the
two cities, we would say of the church what we say of all other
historical communities. It exists as a swaying to and fro between
two ultimate possibilities represented by the two cities. The
church is simply, as Markus puts it, "the world as reconciled and
redeemed."[35] Such a reading has the advantage of not suppos-

---

35. Markus, *Saeculum,* p. 167.

ing that the church can simply be identified with the city God is building, but it has the enormous disadvantage of being able to say very little about the sort of community the church should be — other than, presumably, that it exists as a sign of the *communio* God aims to produce. The price of reading Augustine in such a way that he does not become a progenitor of an idea of "Christendom" is that we read him in a way that makes puzzling his commitment to the internal life of the church and its mission to the world (as anything other or more than a "sign"). It then becomes quite difficult to say, as does Bonhoeffer: "The body of Christ takes up physical space here on earth."[36]

It is therefore essential to note that a conception of the church as "the world as reconciled and redeemed" does not capture fully the place of the church in Augustine's thinking — nor even in his life.[37] "Augustine always thought of himself as living among a new 'people' — the *populus Dei*, the 'people of God,' the direct successors of a compact and distinctive tribe, the 'people of Israel.' It was not for him to inveigh against Roman society as a whole: it was his first duty to look after his own, to maintain the identity and the morale of his 'people,' the Catholic congregation."[38] Moreover, although Au-

36. Dietrich Bonhoeffer, *Discipleship*, Dietrich Bonhoeffer Works, vol. 4 (Minneapolis: Fortress, 2001), p. 225. A little earlier in the same volume Bonhoeffer puts it as follows: "The bond between Jesus and the disciples who followed him was a bodily bond. This was no accident but a necessary consequence of the incarnation. A prophet and teacher would not need followers, but only students and listeners. But the incarnate Son of God who took on human flesh does need a community of followers [*Nachfolgegemeinde*] who not only participate in his teaching but also in his body" (p. 215).

37. Markus himself notes that "Augustine's thought on the 'heavenly city' is not quite parallel to the development of his thought on the 'earthly city'" (*Saeculum*, p. 118).

38. Peter Brown, *Augustine of Hippo* (Berkeley, Los Angeles, and London: University of California Press, 1967), p. 250. Cf. also p. 278: "[I]n Augustine's

gustine sometimes speaks of the two cities as eschatological realities having no clear institutional embodiment in history, at other times he seems to identify the City of God with the church.

At the end of book 1, as Augustine begins to chart the course he will be taking in *City of God,* he characterizes the two cities as "interwoven and intermixed in this era," awaiting "separation at the last judgment." Some who seem to be members of this city, who even "are united with her in participation in the sacraments," will nevertheless "not join with her in the eternal destiny of the saints" (1.35). This characterization, which pictures the cities less as institutions than as collections of individuals (whose ultimate status is hidden from us), Augustine never entirely sets aside. Thus, for example, when in book 15 he begins to set out the history and development of the cities, he describes his task in largely similar terms: "I classify the human race into two branches: the one consists of those who live by human standards, the other of those who live according to God's will. I also call these two classes the two cities, speaking allegorically" (15.1). The "City of the saints" itself "is up above, although it produces citizens here below, and in their persons the City is on pilgrimage until the time of its kingdom comes" (15.1).

Alongside such characterizations, however, must be set quite different ones. Thus, for example, Augustine can write that "the Church, even now [that is, even while on pilgrimage] is the kingdom of Christ and the kingdom of heaven" (20.9). And, indeed, the way he structures his discussion of the simultaneous development of the two cities — as, for example, in

---

middle age, his intellectual progress had come to involve the commitment of the whole personality to the Catholic church."

18.1 — seems clearly to have in mind empirical, sociological realities.[39] Perhaps more important than terminological examination is the fact that for Augustine the church cannot simply be described as — like all other communities — a movement back and forth between two ultimate possibilities. Other communities we may properly describe as open to both cities, but the church is not in the same way open to the *civitas terrena*. The church may be (as we characterized it on the first reading of *City of God* given above) "the world reconciled," but it is also a community set apart from the world. It is not the only place where God is at work in the world, for Augustine is clear that there are some not presently united in the church's sacramental life who will one day be seen to be citizens of the *civitas Dei*. But in its sacramental life the church is the extension of Christ's incarnation, the place where his body continues to be present in human history.

Here again it may be useful to recall what Augustine does in his *Confessions*. There he describes human beings as drawn — by *amor sui* and *amor Dei* — in two ultimate directions. Every human being is so characterized, tugged in those contrary directions — desiring to rest in God but pulled back by the love of other good things. Even Christians, because they are not perfectly sanctified, have divided loves. Nevertheless, Christians are not in bondage the way they were before being set free by God's grace. Before that life-shattering experience in the garden, Augustine experienced himself as caught between two loves, two wills — each of them his. "I . . . was on both sides" (8.5). He simply was the division, caught within it.

39. Cf. also 8.24 ("this house, the City of God, which is the holy Church"); 13.16 ("the City of God, that is to say, God's Church"); 16.2 ("Christ and his Church, which is the City of God").

Nor was the division entirely gone after his experience in the garden; he could still look toward a day "[w]hen in my whole self I shall cling to you united" (10.28). Nevertheless, something decisive had happened when his "heart was filled with a light of confidence" (8.12). Divided his loves remained, but he was no longer on both sides of that division, no longer ruled or governed by it.

Something like that is true of the church. While on pilgrimage it has within its midst those who will finally be seen to belong to the *civitas terrena,* but it does not exist as a community simply caught within the field of force between the two cities. It is not open to the earthly city, as all other historical communities are; it could not ultimately become that city. Hence, the church always exists as a standing alternative to all other societies, including those — such as nations — that make powerful claims upon our loyalty. This is the truth that has come to powerful expression again in John Milbank's reappropriation of Augustine, overstated as it is in places. Milbank is right to see that the church itself has become for Augustine a political reality, though it is less than helpful when Milbank asserts that all political theory is thereby "relocated by Christianity as thought about the church."[40] To take such a claim seriously would be to fail to appreciate the hand of God working through government to fashion a modest peace — indeed, a peace that falls "gratefully upon the ear" (19.11) — which peace, Augustine says, the church gladly uses and (even) "defends and seeks" (19.17) as it makes its way through history. We need not, in order to carve out a distinctive place for the community of the church, deny God's hand in the work of government. Milbank, for example, holds that God engages in no act of

40. Milbank, p. 406.

"judgment" (which is, of course, central to the work of government). "[E]very time we punish, or utter a judgment against someone held in our power, we deny that person's freedom and spiritual equality. . . . This stance of judgment and punishment is *never* occupied by God."[41] Forgetting government for a moment, who would want to spend much time in the company of children who had been raised according to such beliefs? Or in a society that eschewed the very idea of punishment? We should not pass off as theological wisdom views that we would not actually try to live by, nor should we deny that it is God who works through government to preserve the world toward the city he is building.

Such excesses aside, it is true that the church can provide a standing alternative to other societies only insofar as it forms the life of the faithful. Commitment to do that, rather than any counter-ontology, is all we need to see the inadequacy of a view that characterizes the church simply as "the world reconciled." Thus, for example, consider what is missing from Markus's description of the tasks for which the church is "set apart for signifying and pointing to the coming Kingdom."[42] The church is, he writes, to proclaim the gospel, to engage in sacramental worship that provides the "anticipatory sign" of the coming kingdom, and to serve the world.[43] We need quarrel with none of these in order to note what is strikingly absent: forming the lives of believers into a pattern distinctively Christian. Only when and as this is done could the church possibly provide the world with an alternative vision of community.

Thus, we need a way (other than the medieval one) of read-

---

41. Milbank, p. 421.
42. Markus, *Saeculum*, p. 184.
43. Markus, *Saeculum*, p. 185.

ing the two cities not only as eschatological realities but also as historical communities: the earthly city, of which Rome is the exemplar; the City of God, heavenly in its origin and its destination, foreshadowed in history by Israel, and now given historical location in Christ and his body, the church.[44] As opposites, these cities can never be merged in a Christian society (of the sort Augustine himself may have had in mind in an earlier period of his thinking). The only society that can be "Christianized" is the church, and it invites all people to share in its distinctive way of life. Therefore, the church does not exercise political rule, and it should not think of its task primarily as giving advice to rulers. Instead, the church shapes Christian conscience and bears witness to Christian truth — bears witness precisely by entering with its own distinctive language into public argument and debate.

Nevertheless, to the degree that the church is successful in its mission, to the degree that it genuinely forms the life of the faithful in distinctively Christian ways, it may also — even if unwittingly — be reshaping and reforming the surrounding society in ways that are more open to Christian insight and principle. It may form the consciences of those who serve in public life and exercise political rule — and who will know better than to imagine that their faith could be set aside or bracketed when they serve in such ways. Part of the Christian vision they bring to bear in public life will of course be the clear realization that politics is not and should not seek to be redemptive. But well within the boundaries established by that realization there will be room for their "comprehensive doctrines," their vision of what is good

44. Cranz, p. 411. As I noted above, however, Cranz goes too far — and misses the truth in the first reading of the two cities — when he says human societies can have no positive relation whatever to the City of God (cf. n. 6 above).

and truly human, to shape their activity. This will certainly have its dangers, since "any inculturated church is liable to lose its critical distance on society."[45] Yet, what is the alternative? Christians can hardly decline to face such dangers, for, as Oliver O'Donovan has nicely put it, "[t]he church is not at liberty to withdraw from mission; nor may it undertake its mission without confident hope of success."[46]

Indeed, the real bulwark of a sphere of private conscience protected from government coercion turns out in fact to be the church (whose very existence is among the most important historical causes of such liberty in the West). The continued existence of a church intent on being church, intent on offering itself as an alternative community that claims our loyalty, thwarts the pretensions of political rule. In a society where there is such a church, politics can never claim citizens to the whole extent of their being. The best protection of human liberty, of a private realm beyond the proper power of government, is not any concept of "public reason" denuded of religious language and commitment. It is rather the church with its distinctive way of life, determined to bear public witness to its life and to be Christ's Body in the world — whose very presence announces that political rule can never be redemptive and must therefore be limited. Hence, it is no paradox but simple truth to say that only a church set over against the world can be a church for the world. In setting limits to politics, the church points to the God who alone can claim our final allegiance, and it thereby reminds us that no lesser god can claim us wholly and entirely.

45. Oliver O'Donovan, *The Desire of the Nations: Rediscovering the Roots of Political Theology* (Cambridge: Cambridge University Press, 1996), p. 225.
46. O'Donovan, p. 212.

SEX

Politics is not the only realm of life from which we might ask more than it can provide. Desire is at least as at home in areas of life less public and political, more intimate and personal. And just as the search for wholeness or completion within the political realm can become a kind of religious quest, so also can the desire for sexual union. It is no accident that eros is, in its deepest dimension, a longing for the divine. It is important therefore that such pretensions, just as much as our political pretensions, be chastened by duty. Thinking with Augustine — even when we have to correct him, as we will — may help remind us that sexual love is not simply an act of fulfillment or gratification, but also an act of renunciation; for it directs us away from ourselves toward both the loved one and the next generation.

In a world such as ours, in which we are hard pressed to agree on any moral requirement other than consent, it is all too easy to regard the body — especially in its sexual nature — as merely available for our use in the satisfaction of desire. Thinking with Augustine about this is especially helpful, for precisely because he shares (from his quite different angle of vision) some of the defects of our own way of thinking, he may force us to do better.

Despite what undergraduates are often still taught, it is inaccurate to say that the mature Augustine condemned either the body or sexual pleasure. His turn from the Manichees was a real one.[1] What is true, however, is that *desire* for sexual pleasure, at least as fallen human beings experience such desire, was for him deeply suspect. He returns time and again to this issue, especially in his anti-Pelagian writings, but also in other, more general contexts.

Thus, in book 11 of the *City of God,* having completed his long critique of Roman politics and religion, Augustine turns to the origin of the two cities in the creation of angels and then humankind. Death follows upon human sin, but Augustine detours in book 13 to emphasize that when God overcomes death it will be in a risen body, not just in a soul. At the beginning of book 14 he takes pains in several ways to make clear that being "bodily" is not itself a problem. He notes, for example, that the "sins of the flesh" spoken of in the Bible are not only sensual (e.g., lust and drunkenness) but also spiritual (e.g., quarrelsomeness and jealousy). Moreover, sins of the flesh are attributed even to Satan, who of course has no body. Augustine then proceeds in book 14 to reject the Stoic ideal of *apatheia* — as if it were right for us to try to live without experiencing the passions of bodily life. Even though certain emo-

---

1. Kim Power, *Veiled Desire: Augustine on Women* (New York: Continuum, 1996), p. 107: "[T]he criticism that Manichaeism always influenced Augustine to some extent is difficult to support unequivocally." Cf. also Paul Ramsey, "Human Sexuality in the History of Redemption," *Journal of Religious Ethics* 16 (Spring 1988): 60: "Augustine does not say that there is anything shameful about the body, the genital organs or their connection and movement in coitus. What he finds shameful is the operation of sexuality without the personal presence of the man and woman in it."

tions (such as fear) will not exist in heaven, he argues that there would be something inhuman about trying to remove them from this temporal life.

That discussion leads him quite naturally to a consideration of the first, unfallen, human beings in paradise. What passions would they have experienced, and how would their experience have been altered by sin? Here Augustine focuses on sexual desire, arguing that unfallen and properly integrated desire would have been very different from the desire we now experience — and, indeed, that our unintegrated desires are a manifestation of and punishment for sin.

In the long development of Christian thought and institutions, especially within Roman Catholicism, Augustine's deeply influential analysis of sexual desire gave rise to the view that it is wrong to separate the pleasure of the sexual act from the procreative good of marriage. This meant, from one angle, a condemnation of contraception, which makes available the pleasure of the act while simultaneously forestalling the possibility that coitus may result in children. And it meant, from another angle, a condemnation of technologies of assisted reproduction, attempting, as they do, to produce a child apart from coitus.

By thinking with Augustine, I aim to reconsider these questions. Put a little too simply for the moment, I hope to explain where his depiction of contraceptive intercourse goes awry, how it might be corrected, and why, if uncorrected, it might actually lead one to endorse rather than condemn techniques of assisted reproduction. Only, I think, by jettisoning the view of sexual desire that leads Augustine to condemn deliberately nonprocreative coitus is it really possible to make a persuasive case against assisted reproduction. Thus, I hope to dislodge the tight connection that Roman Catholic thought has often seen between these two issues — condemning, as it has, both contraceptive intercourse and assisted reproduction — in order to understand how and why one might approve the first but not the second.

I will take a long way round to this goal, however, beginning, in a sense, where Augustine himself began, with the question: What would sinless, rightly integrated, sexual desire have been like in paradise? And to ask that question with Augustine, it may be useful to start by attending not to sex but to food.

Food

Characterizing Augustine's understanding of the place of rightly ordered pleasure and desire in marriage, Kim Power writes: "[A] man had to love his spouse, but preferably not her body, and both parties were permitted an ordinate sexual pleasure in conjugal relations as long as they were not motivated by desire. This is like saying it is acceptable to enjoy eating, but not to feel hungry."[2] Such a comparison between desire for the pleasures of sex and desire for the pleasures of eating is not at all misplaced in a discussion of Augustine's thought.[3]

---

2. Power, p. 229. Actually, Power's statement is not quite fair to Augustine, or at least to what Augustine sometimes says. He can distinguish hunger from the kind of craving desire that he thinks is wrong. For example, in *Against Julian,* Fathers of the Church, vol. 35 (Washington, D.C.: Catholic University of America Press, 1957), he puts the point as follows: "When nature in its way demands supplements which are absent, we do not say this is lust, but hunger or thirst. When the need has been satisfied, yet the love of eating tempts the soul, then we have lust, then we have the evil to which a man must not yield, but must resist" (4.14.67).

3. The comparison has come naturally to others. See, for example, John C. Cavadini, "Feeling Right: Augustine on the Passions and Sexual Desire," *Au-*

When in his *Confessions* (10.30-41) Augustine begins to take stock of how well he is succeeding in living as a Christian since his conversion, he undertakes an examination of conscience under three rubrics drawn from 1 John 2:16: lust of the flesh (sensual desires), lust of the eyes (intellectual curiosity), and the pride of life (love of praise). His discussion has struck some as insufficiently world-affirming, a criticism nicely stated by Robert O'Connell.

> That examination of conscience makes, surely, some of the most depressing reading in all of Christian literature. There is something profoundly saddening about the portrait it presents: the great Bishop of Hippo tormenting himself about the pleasure he cannot avoid while eating . . . or listening to psalmody . . . ; berating himself that the spectacle of a dog chasing a hare, or of a lizard snaring a fly, can still distract his interest. . . . Even more saddening, perhaps, the thought of Christian generations who have been confused and troubled by the dreadful indictment of those wholesome human things, to say nothing of Christians today and tomorrow who, influenced by pages like these and others following their inspiration, will continue to doubt their own healthy acceptance of the world God made "good," indeed, "very good."[4]

Among those "wholesome human things," as O'Connell notes, is the pleasure we take in eating, and it is undeniable

---

gustinian Studies 36, no. 1 (2005): 196: "*Concupiscentia carnis* is desire disintegrated against will and against itself, not simply an innocent impulse, like hunger though more difficult to use in moderation."

4. Robert J. O'Connell, *St. Augustine's Confessions: The Odyssey of Soul* (Cambridge: Harvard University Press, 1969), p. 133.

that Augustine worries considerably about his own continued desire for food. He articulates a kind of "food as medicine" theory of rightly ordered eating.

> This you have taught me, that I should have the same attitude toward taking food as I have toward taking medicine. But while I pass from the discomfort of hunger to the satisfaction of sufficiency, in that very moment of transition there is set for me a snare of concupiscence. For the moment of transition is pleasurable, and we are forced to go through that moment; there is no other way. And while we eat and drink for the sake of health, there is a dangerous kind of pleasure which follows in attendance on health and very often tries to put itself first, so that what I say that I am doing, and mean to do, for the sake of my health is actually done for the sake of pleasure. Nor is there the same measure for both; what is enough for health is not enough for pleasure, and it is often hard to tell whether it is the necessary care of my body asking for sustenance or whether it is a deceitful voluptuousness of greed trying to seduce me. And because of this uncertainty the unhappy soul is delighted; it uses it as a cover and excuse for itself, and is glad that it is not clearly evident what is sufficient for a healthy moderation, so that under the cloak of health it may hide the business of pleasure. (10.31)

In the purposeful ordering of God's creation food is, Augustine believes, a kind of medicine. The *good* of food, its end or purpose, is that it serves health; it sustains and nourishes life. Such nourishment is for us a necessity. We cannot avoid it, and indeed we must seek it. Even if we discipline our desire for food by fasting, it is still a good that we must sometimes seek. (We might note, though, that Augustine does say in *City of God* [13.22] that the resurrected bodies of the saints in heaven "will eat only if they wish to eat; eating will be for them a possibility, not a necessity." This is worth keeping in mind for my argument yet to be developed. Why might the saints wish to eat in heaven when they have no necessity of doing so? Perhaps to feast. If so, eating must serve some other good in addition to sustaining the health of the body — perhaps some good of human community.)

It happens, however, that, essential as eating is for human beings, "this necessity is sweet" to us.[5] We may easily become its prisoner, for we enjoy eating and often take great pleasure in it. To see the danger here as Augustine sees it, we must distinguish between the *good* of an activity (its appropriate end and purpose) and the *pleasure* the activity gives. There is, on Augustine's view, nothing wrong with taking pleasure in any permitted activity. Wrong enters in only if we seek the pleasure apart from the good.

Because the necessity of eating is sweet to us, we may attempt precisely that — to separate the pleasure of eating from the good of eating. We may seek the pleasure for its own sake, wholly apart from the good. This can happen through sheer overeating, or perhaps more subtly through the refined palate and exquisite sensibilities of the gourmand. If we do, Augustine believes we are wrapping ourselves more firmly in the chains of necessity, and are likely to get an ever diminishing pleasure from an ever increasing devotion to eating.

There are problems with this view, but it is by no means

5. Augustine even notes in *Against Julian* that the necessity *must* be sweet. Were the food we take in not at all tasty or pleasurable, we wouldn't eat it, and the body would not be nourished (4.14.67).

silly. Nor will we get at its deficiencies simply by supposing that its rather severe ascetic outlook fails to appreciate "wholesome human things." At least from the perspective of Augustine's Christian belief, there is something touchingly naive about our supposing that — east of Eden — we are able easily to say what a wholesome and well-integrated desire for food would be like. Nevertheless, defend Augustine as we may, we probably also have a nagging suspicion that something has gone wrong in his analysis of eating — that, necessary as food is for nourishment, the purposes of eating are not exhausted by our need to remain alive. Eating because we are hungry and must take in nourishment to live would of course serve the "good" of eating, in that it would nourish and sustain our bodies, but it would not distinguish us from the other animals. We might think of it more as "feeding" than "eating."[6] There would be no additional and distinctively human good in the enjoyment of the meal.

Consider the subtitle of Leon Kass's book *The Hungry Soul: Eating and the Perfecting of Our Nature.* From Augustine's perspective Kass may seem too ready to depict the perfecting of our nature as within our power, but there is something to be learned from Kass's discussion about the several goods of eating. He depicts a movement first from feeding to eating, as we make of our animal needs the occasion for a distinctively human activity. But even within that human activity we may trace still further movement — from civilized eating structured by manners to noble dining that becomes the occasion for conversation among friends, to a holy feast in which we "cele-

6. Leon R. Kass, *The Hungry Soul: Eating and the Perfecting of Our Nature* (New York: Free Press, 1994), p. 107. In German, for example, the distinction (between *fressen* and *essen*) is more obvious.

brate, in gratitude and reverence, the mysterious source of the articulated world and its generous hospitality in providing food, both for life and for thought."[7]

Enjoying a meal means, in part, enjoying it in the company of others, and there is something about eating together that nourishes human conversation and community. In fact, we must control our desire for more of the food in order to share in that good of eating. Of a "gluttonous eater who, overcome by animal compulsion towards the food that lies before him, ignores the presence of his companion, and sets to like a pig at a trough," we are likely to say that he displays bad manners.[8] Yet, we might almost say more — that he perverts the meaning of eating. In addition to bodily nourishment, the only good of eating discerned by Augustine, Kass characterizes "the higher and deeper yearnings" of our nature in a way that captures what we can call only another *good* of eating: "pointings toward community and friendship (encouraged by gracious manners and the adornments of the table); pointings toward discernment and understanding (encouraged by tasteful dining and lively conversation); and yearnings for a relation to the divine (encouraged by a ritual sanctification of the meal)."[9]

All this has its ground, of course, in human necessity. We must eat to live. Kass's account does not denigrate this ground; indeed, it accentuates and affirms it, acknowledging and approving our animality. Nevertheless, the good of eating is also something more than satisfying hunger or preserving life. This deeper, distinctively human, good is experienced not as something external to eating — not as an end to which eat-

7. Kass, p. 198.
8. Roger Scruton, *Sexual Desire: A Moral Philosophy of the Erotic* (New York: Free Press, 1986), p. 289.
9. Kass, p. 228.

ing is a means — but in and through the meal itself. The necessity of eating is sweet, but for reasons rather different from those that impressed themselves upon Augustine. "Necessity — our bodily neediness — cannot only be humanized; meeting it knowingly and deliberately can also be humanizing. For those who understand both the meaning of eating and their own hungry soul, necessity becomes the mother of the specifically human virtues: freedom, sympathy, moderation, beautification, taste, liberality, tact, grace, wit, gratitude, and, finally, reverence."[10]

Augustine's analysis of the good of eating is not so much wrong, therefore, as it is incomplete. The biological good of eating is indeed that it nourishes our life, and there is no doubt that eating gives a pleasure that may be separated from that good and sought for its own sake — sought, even, in ways that could ultimately undermine the good of health. But as a human activity, eating also realizes another, more complicated good — the human community that a shared meal can constitute. Thus, eating serves two purposes: it nourishes our bodily life, and it incarnates conversation and community. A life that lacked either good of eating would lack something important and significant for human life.

This does not mean, of course, that both purposes must be served every time we eat. Sometimes these goods are held

10. Kass, p. 229. Let us give Augustine his due even here, however. It may sometimes — often? — be hard to know whether we are simply delighting in the good of civilized eating, noble dining, and holy feasting *or* enjoying the thought of ourselves as people capable of doing so. No one sees more clearly than Augustine how deeply buried within us is the power of self-deception and how difficult — finally impossible — it is for us to know ourselves as we truly are. What began in the necessity of feeding and was transformed into human eating (dining and feasting) may become a new necessity that wraps us in the "sweetness" of its own chains.

closely together in an act of eating; at other times they are not. I may eat by myself, simply because I am hungry and need nourishment. I may share a meal with others for the sake of their company even when I am not hungry and have no need of nourishment. To separate the goods of eating in such ways does not necessarily dishonor or turn against either. One could, to be sure, separate these goods in ways that would be evil. One could feast so often and so sumptuously with friends that one's health was harmed, or one could eat only to stay alive, regularly declining the invitation to fellowship that a shared meal can occasion. But not every separation of the goods of eating goes wrong in such ways. We must look at any such separation in all its particularity in order to judge its moral reality.

Sex

Describing Augustine's vision of God's plan to sustain the human race through procreation, Donald X. Burt, O.S.A., writes: "In order to implement this plan, God made human beings with a strong desire for coitus. Just as hunger and thirst were given so that humans could maintain their health, so the impulse towards physical intercourse was given to insure the health of the race. And just as the pleasure from satisfied hunger and thirst is made noble by the good end that it accomplishes, so too the passion that accompanies intercourse is made holy by the great good that the act can accomplish, the formation of new human beings in a crucible of love."[11] This is too sympathetic a reading of Augustine, but the connection

11. Donald X. Burt, O.S.A., *Friendship and Society: An Introduction to Augustine's Practical Philosophy* (Grand Rapids: Eerdmans, 1999), p. 82.

Burt discerns is really there in Augustine's thinking. He treats sexual desire almost exactly as he treats the desire for food. Even as one should come to the table to eat when one's body needs nourishment, so also would our first parents have come to the marriage bed when children were needed. "I do not see," Augustine writes, "what could have prohibited them from honorable nuptial union and *the bed undefiled* even in Paradise. God could have granted them this if they had lived in a faithful and just manner in obedience and holy service to Him, so that without the tumultuous ardor of passion . . . offspring would be born from their seed."[12] Before we consider how this understanding of the purpose of sex — like Augustine's understanding of the purpose of food — may be incomplete and inadequate, we should try to take it seriously. To that end we can consider an image of sexuality that depicts it in something like Augustine's way — as having a particular *good* or purpose, which good we might easily separate from the *pleasure* it gives, and come to seek the pleasure alone.

In *Out of the Silent Planet*, the first of C. S. Lewis's space fantasies, the protagonist Ransom finds himself on the planet Malacandra, where three species of *hnau* — *sorns*, *pfifltriggi*, and *hrossa* — live together in peace under the rule of Maleldil. To learn more about Malacandra, Ransom spends time talking with Hyoi, one of the *hrossa*. Their conversation turns at one point to continuation of the species. Is there ever danger on

---

12. Saint Augustine, *The Literal Meaning of Genesis, Volume II*, Ancient Christian Writers, no. 42 (New York and Ramsey, N.J.: Newman, 1982), 9.3. Similarly, in *City of God* (14.24) Augustine writes: "Then (had there been no sin) the man would have sowed the seed and the woman would have conceived the child when their sexual organs had been aroused by the will, at the appropriate time and in the necessary degree, and had not been excited by lust."

Malacandra that the population of *hrossa* might outstrip food production? The question is almost unintelligible to Hyoi. He cannot understand why they might produce that many off-spring.

Ransom found this difficult. At last he said:

"Is the begetting of young not a pleasure among the *hrossa?*"

"A very great one, *Hmān*. This is what we call love."

"If a thing is a pleasure, a *hmān* wants it again. He might want the pleasure more often than the number of young that could be fed."

It took Hyoi a long time to get the point.

"You mean," he said slowly, "that he might do it not only in one or two years of his life but again?"

"Yes."

"But why? Would he want his dinner all day or want to sleep after he had slept? I do not understand."

"But a dinner comes every day. This love, you say, comes only once while the *hross* lives?"

"But it takes his whole life. When he is young he has to look for his mate; and then he has to court her; then he be-gets young; then he rears them; then he remembers all this, and boils it inside him and makes it into poems and wisdom."

"But the pleasure he must be content only to remember?"

"That is like saying, 'My food I must be content to eat.'"[13]

13. C. S. Lewis, *Out of the Silent Planet* (New York: Macmillan, 1965), pp. 72-73.

This is of course Augustine's "food as medicine" approach to sex; yet, I have to say that in Hyoi's mouth it does not seem all that strange. On Malacandra it makes sense. Malacandra is an unfallen world, and we are prepared to consider the possibility that rightly ordered sexual desire in such a world might be quite different from our own experience. Why would someone want to keep grasping at this pleasure forever when the good of offspring had been satisfied? Indeed, pondering his discovery of "a species naturally continent, naturally monogamous," Ransom is led to doubt the usefulness of our fallen sexuality as a guide to right order: "At last it dawned upon him that it was not they, but his own species, that were the puzzle."[14]

In *Mere Christianity* Lewis applied such thinking not to an unfallen world but to our own, the "silent planet." "You can get a large audience together for a strip-tease act — that is, to watch a girl undress on the stage. Now suppose you came to a country where you could fill a theatre by simply bringing a covered plate on to the stage and then slowly lifting the cover so as to let every one see, just before the lights went out, that it contained a mutton chop or a bit of bacon, would you not think that in that country something had gone wrong with the appetite for food?"[15] Likewise, Lewis suggests, pressing the analogy, might not a visitor from a different world think that something had gone wrong with sexual desire in our world? Thus, whether we begin with an imaginative unfallen world or with the clear disorder of our own world, we may learn to be cautious about supposing that we can take our own sexual experience as a guide to right order. That is what taking Augustine seriously can do for us. "There are . . . men at the present time

14. Lewis, *Silent Planet*, p. 74.
15. C. S. Lewis, *Mere Christianity* (New York: Macmillan, 1960), p. 75.

who are evidently unaware of the bliss that existed in paradise. They suppose that children could not have been begotten except by the means with which they are familiar, namely, by means of lust."[16]

We can by now begin to connect the dots, and in so doing note that we have reconstructed what in general outline is the original shape of the Roman Catholic case against contraception (in the development of which Augustine was, of course, of incalculable importance). The argument, simply put, is: the *good* or purpose of marriage is procreation — production of offspring. To be sure, sexual intercourse also gives pleasure, and there is nothing wrong with that. Indeed, it would have given pleasure even to Adam and Eve in paradise.[17] But if we come to seek the pleasure alone — apart from the purpose for which our sexuality is intended — we have distorted our nature. Contraceptive intercourse is an attempt to separate the pleasure of the act from its good. Adam and Eve in paradise would not have so separated this pleasure from this good. They would have engaged in sexual intercourse "as a deliberate act undisturbed by human passion" for the purpose only of producing children — and they would have enjoyed, as a kind of bonus, the pleasure the act also gives.[18] We should not underestimate what Augustine here grants. He was, in Peter Brown's words, "quite prepared to allow that such [sexual] pleasure might have occurred in Paradise — no small imaginative feat for a late antique per-

16. *City of God* 14.21. Cf. Cavadini, p. 204: "[I]f it is accepted that lust is a pathologized desire, trying to imagine sex without lust is not the same thing as trying to imagine sex without feeling, even intense feeling."

17. Cf. Power, p. 106: "It is important to note that what Augustine repudiated was not desire *per se*, nor pleasure, but inordinate desire and pleasure not controlled by the will."

18. *City of God* 14.26. Cf. also Ramsey, pp. 60-62.

son of ascetic lifestyle. What concerned him was that, after the fall of Adam and Eve, this pleasure had gained a momentum of its own."[19] Augustine's worry, that is, was that as the search for this pleasure becomes a sweet necessity, we may attempt to separate the pleasure of the act from the good of procreation, seeking the pleasure for its own sake alone.

We may, then, summarize Augustine's view — or at least, one reasonable reading of it — as follows: just as nourishment constitutes the good of food, the eating of which also, as it happens, gives pleasure, so children constitute the good of sex, the experience of which also, as it happens, gives pleasure. As we should not grasp for the pleasure of eating apart from the good purpose to which it is divinely ordered, so also we should not seek the pleasure of the sexual act apart from the good to which it is divinely ordered. Food is medicine — that is, its purpose is our sustenance and health. Sexual intercourse is also a kind of medicine: it sustains not the individual but the species. Its purpose is offspring.

Food and Sex

When thinking with Augustine about the pleasures and dangers of food, we found it necessary in the end to move toward a richer and deeper understanding than his of the good of eating as a human activity. We must do the same in the case of sex. Indeed, Roman Catholic thought itself — though its condemnation of contraceptive intercourse had roots in the Augustinian contention that the pleasure of sex and the good of off-

19. Peter Brown, *The Body and Society: Men, Women, and Sexual Renunciation in Early Christianity* (New York: Columbia University Press, 1988), p. 417.

spring are not to be separated — has not been able to rest entirely content with his analysis. Having thought with Augustine about the place of food and of sex in human life, we need to bring these together and see what can be learned from the one for the other. Even in Augustine's day the monk Jovinian, who was condemned (whether rightly or wrongly has been disputed) for teaching that virginity and marriage were equally worthy states of life, extended his critique to the use of food, teaching that "[t]here is no difference between abstinence from food and receiving it with thanksgiving."[20] And, of course, Augustine's experience as a Manichee would have suggested an ascetic practice that connected abstinence from sex with abstinence from food.[21] Insight gained in the one case (food) may help in the other (sex).

In his instructive assessment of Augustine's understanding of human sexuality in the history of redemption, Paul Ramsey suggested that Augustine had "the problem of saying why only one tumult of the soul — that which springs from fallen sexuality — causes shame."[22] Ramsey was of course right to note that Augustine placed great argumentative emphasis on man's inability to control his generative organ and the shame that inability created. Nevertheless, the kind of description Augustine gives of sin's effect on sexuality is not unlike language he uses in other contexts. For example, he sees in the unruliness of the sexual organ an apt punishment for man's disobedience to God. In *City of God* (16.4) he uses similar language to describe the scattering of the peoples at the Tower of Babel:

20. David G. Hunter, "Resistance to the Virginal Ideal in Late-Fourth-Century Rome: The Case of Jovinian," *Theological Studies* 48 (March 1987): 51.

21. Hunter, p. 53.

22. Ramsey, p. 63.

"Since a ruler's power of domination is wielded by his tongue, it was in that organ that his pride was condemned to punishment. And the consequence was that he who refused to understand God's bidding so as to obey it, was himself not understood when he gave orders to men." Closer still to my concern, when Augustine speaks of the need to discipline the body by fasting, he says: "Your flesh is below you; above you is your God. When you wish your flesh to serve you, you are reminded of how it is fitting for you to serve your God."[23] Other desires — in particular, our desire for food — are, like sex, necessities that may in our bondage to sin become sweet to us. To consider together these two necessities, sex and food, offers an occasion to do for sex what we did for food — namely, to find in it another good beyond the obvious biological one.

I suggested above that Augustine's analysis of our desire for food was incomplete in an important way. Eating serves, in his view, only one good: nourishment of life and health. Any legitimate pleasure we have in eating may not therefore be separated from and pursued apart from that good. We should eat only to sustain life. What Augustine missed, I suggested, was another good that eating serves — the human conversation and community that a shared meal constitutes. Perhaps we should wonder whether something similar is not missing from his analysis of sexual desire. He supposed that in paradise the bond joining Adam and Eve would have been essentially a bond of concord or friendship. "Their married intercourse, had it occurred, would have been [merely and no more than] a physical concretization of their pre-existing concord."

23. Augustine, "The Usefulness of Fasting," in *Saint Augustine: Treatises on Various Subjects*, Fathers of the Church, vol. 16 (Washington, D.C.: Catholic University of America Press, 1952), p. 4.

Hence, he "never found a way . . . of articulating the possibility that sexual pleasure might, in itself, enrich the relations between husband and wife."[24]

Desire for coitus may be put in service of the good of procreation, and we should affirm Augustine's belief — shared generally by Christians — that such procreation is an important good or purpose of sexual union. But sexual desire also embodies, nurtures, and enriches the good of carnal conversation and community — the complete sharing of life — between husband and wife. To seek such community, therefore, even when children are not planned, wanted, or desired, is not mere grasping for a repeated pleasure separated from the good of marriage. On the contrary, it *is* one of the goods of marriage. Thus, contraceptive intercourse for the expression and enjoyment of such community cannot separate the pleasure from the good of marriage; for it *is* one of the goods of marriage.

This brings us, of course, to where Catholic thought itself has in recent years come — to speaking of two goods, procreative and unitive, that marriage serves. For Augustine there was (in paradise) one good of marriage, and the pleasure of the sexual act was not to be separated from that good. Other goods of marriage (fidelity and sacrament) come into the picture only within a fallen world, and they do not alter the basic structure of his thought. To suggest, as I now have, that we should think of sexual union within marriage as itself one of the goods of marriage (rather than simply as a pleasure that must be enjoyed only as part of an act aimed at procreation) is to speak of both a procreative and a unitive good of marriage. So the question we found in Augustine must be reformulated. We now have to ask not about the relation between the pleasure of co-

24. Brown, p. 402.

itus and the good of offspring, but rather about the relation between two goods: children and fleshly communion.

Might contraceptive intercourse wrongly separate not a pleasure from a good but the good of procreation from the good of
communion in love between spouses? The claim that these two
goods must be "inseparable" in the sexual act is essentially the
claim that contraceptive intercourse makes impossible the full
communion in love that the act of coitus between husband and
wife intends. When pondering this claim, we should not forget
what we learned from thinking about the goods of eating. A
meal is both medicine for the body and the expression of human community. In any proposed separation of these goods we
must simply try to see whether the resulting moral reality involves distortion or harm. To express marital communion in
the sexual act while using contraceptives is not unlike sharing
in a festive meal when one is not hungry and eats little. Precisely in order to share fully in the good of community on that
occasion one does not do what one does on the occasion of
some other meals. Although the species-sustaining, biological
purpose of food is not served by such eating, neither of the
goods of eating seems distorted by doing so.

Thus, thinking along with Augustine, we move beyond and
in some respects "correct" his understanding of the place of
both food and sex in human life. We may share in a meal not
to sustain life or health but simply as an embodiment of human community — a kind of "ecstatic" experience in which we
set to the side our aim of self-preservation and simply enter
into the fellowship the meal constitutes. The good not served
in such participation in the meal is not the only good of eating,
and one might well eat even when nourishment is not at all
needed. Likewise, husband and wife may share in the act of
love not to produce a child but simply as the most intimate in-

carnation of their mutual self-giving — a kind of ecstatic experience in which they set aside their procreative potential and simply share the fellowship their bodily union constitutes. The good not served in their coitus is not the only good the sexual act serves, and they might well make love even when they neither need nor desire children. To be sure, deliberately avoiding children indefinitely could be expected to have a subtle but deformative effect on the character of their love. Were this to happen, then, clearly the several goods of marriage would have been separated too greatly.

The implications of such a correction of Augustine's understanding go far beyond a consideration of contraception alone. Indeed, correcting Augustine in this way is necessary if we are to make sense of the deepest reasons for concern about new reproductive technologies — a concern clearly reflected in Catholic teaching. When the Congregation for the Doctrine of the Faith published *Donum Vitae*, central to its rejection of laboratory fertilization was the belief that the child must be understood as gift, not product — equal in dignity to his parents. "[T]he origin of a human person is the result of an act of giving. The one conceived must be the fruit of his parents' love. He cannot be desired or conceived as the product of an intervention of medical or biological techniques."[25]

It is not unusual to see a link between this reasoning, which condemns assisted reproduction, and the reasoning that disapproves of contraception. Certainly the Congregation thought it saw a connection. "Contraception deliberately deprives the conjugal act of its openness to procreation and in this way

---

25. Congregation for the Doctrine of the Faith, *Instruction on Respect for Human Life in Its Origin, and on the Dignity of Procreation* (Boston: St. Paul Books and Media, 1987), p. 28.

brings about a voluntary dissociation of the ends of marriage. Homologous artificial fertilization, in seeking a procreation which is not the fruit of a specific act of conjugal union, objectively effects an analogous separation."[26] More colloquially put, contraception makes possible sex without babies; assisted reproduction makes possible babies without sex. In either case the goods of marriage are separated.

But are the moral realities reflected in these two separations really so similar? Kim Power has claimed that "Augustine implicitly legitimated a split between love and sex which facilitates the depersonalisation of sexual intercourse."[27] This does not, I think, put the matter quite rightly, but she has pointed to a serious problem. Augustine's mistake, as Paul Ramsey noted with characteristic insight, was not that he depersonalized sexual intercourse; it was that he could think of personal presence in only one way. He thought of the person as present in coitus only if the act was undertaken at the command of the rational will (for, presumably, the purpose of procreation).[28] Thus, rightly ordered sexual intercourse would not be depersonalized, but the person present in it would be characterized not in terms of passion but in terms only of reason and will. Even in paradise, says Augustine, "the man would have sowed the seed and the woman would have conceived the child when their sexual organs had been aroused by the will, at the appropriate time and in the necessary degree."[29]

Hence, by his own lights and in terms of his own understanding of the human person, Augustine did not depersonalize sexual activity. Nevertheless, by driving a wedge between

26. Congregation for the Doctrine of the Faith, p. 27.
27. Power, p. 161.
28. Ramsey, pp. 60, 62, 65.
29. *City of God* 14.24.

the desire to give oneself lovingly and passionately in the sexual act and the (rationally willed) purpose of producing a child, he invites us to think of the child as a product. Adam and Eve would, rationally and deliberately, have set to work to produce children as needed, and they would not have consummated their sexual union for any other reason. This is precisely the separation of babies from sexual love, the understanding of the child as product, that new reproductive technologies express. It is just such a separation — what Power calls the "split between love and sex" — that makes many of the new reproductive technologies seem quite reasonable to their advocates. And the case against such forms of reproduction will depend, finally, on a view of personal presence in coitus that Augustine — acknowledging only the good of procreation and not also the good of communion in the sexual act — was unable to develop. But once, unlike Augustine, we acknowledge both procreative and unitive goods in marriage, we are freed to consider the relation — and the separation — of these goods in new ways. Thinking along with Augustine, of the desire for sex as rather like the desire for food, we were able earlier to see why contraception does not necessarily distort or deform the meaning of our sexuality. The separation effected by new reproductive technologies is a different moral reality, however, and we will see what is problematic about it most clearly when we correct Augustine's vision of coitus as nothing more than a rational activity aimed at offspring.

The act of love is not simply a rational, willed undertaking. Of course, a man and a woman might decide to make love. They might choose to do it for certain reasons — for example, because they hope for a child. But in the act itself, passion, not reason or will, is central. We speak of lovers experiencing "ecstasy" — a word that describes a going out of oneself, a relin-

quishing of control, a setting aside of one's projects and purposes. Even if spouses make love because they want a child,
the act itself requires a letting go of such plans and projects in
mutual self-giving. We might even say then, as Ramsey did in
his discussion of Augustine, that "bodily powers and precisely
the spontaneous and rationally insubordinate movements of
sexuality are, for the purpose of accessibility or presence to another being in this world, superior to the means the soul has
for the deliberate communication of itself to the other."[30]
Thus, married intercourse is not merely the concretization of
an already existing concord, which concretization might then
also be put in service of the production of children. On the
contrary, it is a mode of presence to the spouse unlike any
other.

From this act, in the doing of which lovers have set aside all
plans and projects, a child may result. That child — begotten,
not made — springs from their embrace but is not the product
of a purposive act. Such a child may properly be thought of as a
gift. Love-giving has been life-giving, not because the lovers
willed it, but because God has so blessed it. In this instance,
unlike the instance of contraception, the moral reality — our
understanding of the relation of parents and child — does
seem to be distorted if we separate unitive and procreative
goods; the presence of the child then results from our will and
choice. By contrast, the child is a gift precisely because he or
she results from an act and embrace in which we set aside our
intentions and purposes, in which we step out of ourselves and
cease attempting to be productive.

We can begin to see this only as we think our way into Augustine's view and beyond it, recognizing that the act of love

---

30. Ramsey, p. 65.

need not be sought or desired for any reason other than the communion it expresses and embodies. "Producing" a child in other ways seems to distort the moral meaning of the child; it removes the procreative good of marriage from the context in which it is personalized and humanized (and is rather like taking in nourishment entirely apart from the fellowship of the meal). By contrast, within a marriage that is genuinely open to children, embodying the communion of marital love in contraceptive intercourse (rather like sharing in a festive meal while actually eating little and taking in little nourishment) does not in and of itself depersonalize or dehumanize either that act or the child who may be given through it.

All this said, however, we should not fail to give Augustine his due. What he did see, and what his emphasis on procreation might remind us also to see, is that sexuality is more than a personally fulfilling undertaking intended to make us happy and give us pleasure. Of course, the unitive good of marriage is not properly understood when thought of in so self-serving a way, but perhaps it lends itself readily to such distortion. The notion that sexuality is a profound but very private and personal form of play is quite strong in our culture — and that "necessity" becomes sweet to us. By contrast, Augustine saw in the exercise of our sexuality a task — of begetting and rearing children — that God sets before human beings. If in correcting or supplementing his views we lose or ignore that insight, we may ourselves turn out to need correction.

GRIEF

To retrace succinctly the steps that have brought us to this chapter is to see why the subject of grief deserves attention. Our desire to live the "happy" life — which is ultimately the desire for God — may sometimes seem to conflict with our duties. It may appear that doing what is right is more likely to frustrate our desires than to bring them to fruition and fulfillment. This means that within human history we are unlikely to unify the moral life — unlikely to make the duties that obligate us cohere entirely with the goods for which we hope. Life is marked, therefore, by brokenness and incompleteness. Sometimes we look to politics to overcome this brokenness; indeed, we are often tempted to ask of politics more than it can provide. But it never really satisfies the heart's desire for wholeness. We may also turn to more intimate realms of life, most often to sexual love, in search of the fulfillment absent elsewhere. Carefully considered, however, it requires renunciation of personal satisfaction, as it directs us away from ourselves and toward others: toward the loved one, and toward the next generation, which springs from the embrace of mutual love. Indeed, those intimate ties are themselves reminders of life's incompleteness, for when we cannot sustain them we experience grief.

Readers of *The Last Battle,* the seventh and last of C. S. Lewis's Chronicles of Narnia, are given a moving example of the naturalness of grief when Aslan says, "Now make an end," and the magical land of Narnia becomes lifeless and dark. The Pevensie children, who had been kings and queens in Narnia, now find themselves in an even better world of sunlight, flowers, and laughter — Aslan's world. Yet, Peter notices that Lucy is crying.

> "So," said Peter, "Night falls on Narnia. What, Lucy! You're not *crying*? With Aslan ahead, and all of us here?"
>
> "Don't try to stop me, Peter," said Lucy, "I am sure Aslan would not. I am sure it is not wrong to mourn for Narnia. Think of all that lies dead and frozen behind that door."

Then Tirian, last of the kings of Narnia, who is with the children in Aslan's world, comes to Lucy's defense.

> "Sirs," said Tirian. "The ladies do well to weep. See, I do so myself. I have seen my mother's death. What world but Narnia have I ever known? It were no virtue, but great discourtesy, if we did not mourn."[1]

A curious feature of this exchange is that it takes place when the children are in Aslan's world — the Narnian analogue of heaven. It is surprising that they should still experience grief there, but this is perhaps to be explained by the fact that they

---

1. C. S. Lewis, *The Last Battle* (New York: Macmillan, 1956), pp. 149-50.

have only just passed through the stable door from Narnia into Aslan's world, have not yet seen Aslan there face-to-face, and have not yet gone "further up and further in" that world.

In chapter 1, I discussed briefly the place of grief in this life, but I did so primarily in order to worry about a different matter: how heaven can be a world of love if grief is impossible there. For how can attachment in love be genuine if it risks no loss and suffers not at the loss of a loved one? Focusing on whether a God who leaves no place for such grief is a totalitarian God, I noted briefly that in his mature thought Augustine had come to see the inevitability and usefulness of grief in our earthly pilgrimage. We return to that topic now, no longer to think about heaven, but to ponder the place of grief and sorrow in this life.

It would not be hard, after all, to take from Augustine the lesson that earthly life counts for relatively little — and that therefore its loss should have little effect on us. "Smoke has no weight," he writes in *City of God* (5.17) with specific reference to the honor and glory Roman men desired, but with more general reference to all those human goods upon which we set our hearts. And how contrary to our tendency to place our hopes in the political, yet how characteristically Augustinian in some respects, is the Augustine who can write (again in 5.17): "As for this mortal life, which ends after a few days' course, what does it matter under whose rule a man lives, being so soon to die, provided that the rulers do not force him to impious and wicked acts?" Couple a passage such as that with his conviction in the *Confessions* that conversion required him to give up any plan for marriage, highlight these passages for students reading Augustine, and the conclusion follows as surely as the night the day: earthly life, with its ties and attachments, doesn't count for much; hence, losing it should scarcely be cause for grief.

The Sweetness of Life

We should resist this reading of Augustine — not because it is entirely wrong, but because it is far from entirely right. It may therefore be useful to begin by noting some contrary evidence.

Among the most famous sections of the *Confessions* is Augustine's discussion in book 4 of the death of an unnamed friend — an experience that darkened every moment, every place, and every pleasure of life for the young Augustine. Puzzling over the experience, Augustine concludes at one point that his mistake must have been that he had poured out his soul "like water onto sand by loving a man who was bound to die just as if he were an immortal" (4.8). He was stricken with sorrow, because "so is every soul unhappy which is tied to its love for mortal things" (4.6). It is not surprising that many have read this discussion of the death of a friend as a recommendation that, to avoid the perturbations of grief, we should attach ourselves only to God and not to earthly things — and should count as of relatively little importance any earthly attachment that might be lost against one's will. "There [in God] fix your dwelling place, my soul. . . . Entrust to truth whatever truth has given you, and you will lose nothing" (4.11).

The famous discussion in book 4 is to some extent counterbalanced by events recounted in book 9. There Augustine tells of the deaths of his friends Verecundus and Nebridius; of his son, Adeodatus; and — most famously — of his mother, Monica. Grief Augustine certainly experiences, but it is now grief for those he has begun to love "in God," not the inconsolable (and, hence, idolatrous) grief he had recounted in book 4. This is a grief one need not shun or seek to eliminate from life. Kim Paffenroth writes that book 9 provides "the climax and resolution to his crisis over friendship begun in Book Four, and the beginning of a new, more healthy, and more sanctifying conception of earthly attachments."[2] This may state the case for growth too strongly, for there are certainly ambiguities remaining in Augustine's account of his grief at Monica's death. Although he eventually allowed the tears he "had been holding back to fall," he does worry that his may have been "a too carnal affection" (9.12, 13). Still, it would be wrong to say he writes as if the loss of one's mother (or friend or son) should not be cause for grief.[3]

If Augustine's hesitations in book 4 about the appropriateness of grief are somewhat overcome in book 9, more striking still is his brief account in *City of God* of the sorrows friendship inevitably brings in its wake. In the midst of the anxieties of life, Augustine says, the mutual affection of friends is one great consolation. "Yet the more friends we have and the more dispersed they are in different places, the further and more widely extend our fears that some evil may befall them" (19.8). And when this happens — when friends suffer harm, or become enemies rather than friends, or die — we quite rightly grieve.

2. Kim Paffenroth, "Book Nine: The Emotional Heart of the *Confessions*," in *A Reader's Companion to Augustine's "Confessions,"* ed. Kim Paffenroth and Robert P. Kennedy (Louisville and London: Westminster John Knox, 2003), p. 147.

3. For some nuances that Paffenroth does not note, see William Werpehowski, "Weeping at the Death of Dido: Sorrow, Virtue, and Augustine's *Confessions*," *Journal of Religious Ethics* 19 (Spring 1991). Thus, for example, while granting that Augustine's stance in book 9 is more like "patience" than "insensibility," Werpehowski notes that Monica is now described less as a mother than as a sister and friend in the faith. "The embodied and worldly tie between mother and son gives way to a mode of spiritual friendship that seems to overwhelm the former bond" (p. 186).

For if their life brought us the consoling delights of friendship, how could it be that their death should bring us no sadness? Anyone who forbids such sadness must forbid, if he can, all friendly conversation, must lay a ban on all friendly feeling or put a stop to it, must with a ruthless insensibility break the ties of all human relationships, or else decree that they must only be engaged upon so long as they inspire no delight in a man's soul. But if this is beyond all possibility, how can it be that a man's death should not be bitter if his life is sweet to us? (19.8)

If this grief is appropriate, it must be that life is sweet. And if life is sweet, its great goods cannot be thought entirely unworthy of our love.

More generally it is right, I think, to say that *City of God,* in quite different ways at its beginning and its end, teaches that we would be mistaken to regard earthly life as of no account. This is made clear, even if in a seemingly anomalous manner, in Augustine's discussion of suicide in book 1. Even though he believes that this life can hardly be compared with the life in store for citizens of the *civitas Dei,* suicide is forbidden. We should not try to rush ahead to the next, and better, life. But why not? If that better life is our goal, and if in this life we are exposed to many temptations that may keep us from reaching the goal, why not? Why "do we spend time on those exhortations to the newly baptized . . . if we can persuade them to rush to a self-inflicted death immediately upon receiving remission of sins" (1.27)?

We are likely to find the argument amusing, and Augustine in a sense intends that we should; yet, his point is a serious one. It cannot be that only a future life of rest in God counts. On the contrary, a way must be traversed — a way that has its own integrity and importance. This way is not everything, of course. It has worth not simply in itself but because it participates and shares in God's goodness. And for us this way is a school of virtue. The servants of God "have no reason to regret even this life of time, for in it they are schooled for eternity. They enjoy their earthly blessings in the manner of pilgrims and are not attached to them" (1.29). If this sounds like insufficient attachment, that may only be an indication that we prefer to think of this life as freestanding — which to Augustine would sound idolatrous.

Near the end of *City of God* Augustine comes back (in 22.24) to the importance of earthly life, and he does so in a way that may strike us as more genuine appreciation for the sweetness of life. To be sure, even here his purpose is not simply to note the many good things in life. It is rather to impress upon us how wonderful heaven will be if earthly life, which must pale in comparison, is so good. And it is good. The goodness of God "has filled even this misery with innumerable blessings." And then, in some moving paragraphs, Augustine provides what he calls "a kind of compressed pile of blessings," at which he invites us to marvel: arts, inventions, agriculture, navigation, the beauties of different kinds of weather, spices that delight the palate (this from the Augustine who worried about our desire for food), delightful music (this from the Augustine who had worried that music might detract attention from the words of psalmody), the varieties of birds, the activities of ants and bees, the "welcome alternation of day and night," the human being's erect posture, and — my personal favorite — "the brilliant wit shown by philosophers and heretics in defending their very errors and falsehoods." Nor is this "compressed pile of blessings" by any means an adequate account of the goodness of our world. "If I decided to take them singly, to unwrap each one, as it were, and examine it, with all the detailed blessings contained within it, what a time it would take!" But, of course, one should never detach this earthly life from the God who gives it and toward whom it moves — and so Augustine draws the moral of this catalogue of blessings: "And these are all the consolations of mankind under condemnation, not the rewards of the blessed. What then will those rewards be, if the consolations are so many and so wonderful?"

If we pay insufficient heed to this side of Augustine, we will miss the complexity of his assessment of earthly life — and grief at the loss of created things or persons will always seem misplaced. J. N. Figgis, in an insightful passage from his classic discussion of *City of God,* captured well this complexity.

In Augustine there were struggling two men, like Esau and Jacob in the womb of Rebecca. There was Augustine of Thagaste, of Madaura, of Carthage, of Rome, of Milan, the brilliant boy, the splendid and expansive youthful leader, "skilled in all the wisdom of the Egyptians," possessed of the antique culture, rhetorical, dialectic, Roman — the man of the world, the developed humanist with enough tincture of Platonism to gild the humanism; and there is the Augustine of the "Confessions," of the "Sermons," of the "De Civitate," the monk, the ascetic, the otherworldly preacher, the biblical expositor, the mortified priest. These two beings struggle for ever within him, the natural man filled with the sense of beauty and the joy of living, expansive, passionate, artful — and the supernatural Christian fleeing from the world, shunning it, burning what he adored, and adoring what he burnt, celibate and (at times) almost anti-social.[4]

4. J. N. Figgis, *The Political Aspects of St. Augustine's "City of God"* (London: Longmans, Green, and Co., 1921), p. 114.

It is important to do what we can to resolve and clarify this conflict, but thinking with Augustine about the sweetness of life and the appropriateness of grief at loss requires also that we not set aside too quickly the struggle between these "two men."

Appropriate Grief

The opening chapters of book 14 of *City of God* enunciate Augustine's turn away from and against the ancient (especially Stoic) ideal of passionlessness. Of the four "disturbances" of the soul delineated by the ancients — desire, joy, fear, and grief — the one emotion for which the Stoics could find no suitable version or replacement within the wise man's life (of *apatheia*) was grief. For "grief is occasioned by evil which has already happened; and since they think that no evil can happen to a wise man, they have asserted that there can be no corresponding emotion in a wise man's mind" (14.8). Whatever the philosophical complications, Augustine cannot accept such a view for the simple reason that human emotion "was not illusory" in Jesus, "when the Lord himself condescended to live a human life" (14.9). He suffered grief when his message was rejected by his people; he shed tears of sorrow at the death of Lazarus. "Christ's human emotions, as a function of the charity and compassion of God, are . . . not in any way alienated from himself" and are "perfectly integrated acts of the self in love and humility."[5] It must therefore be the case that these emotions — even grief — are appropriate in earthly life "when they are exhibited in the proper situation" (14.9).

5. John C. Cavadini, "Feeling Right: Augustine on the Passions and Sexual Desire," *Augustinian Studies* 36, no. 1 (2005): 202-3.

It is true, as we noted in chapter 1, that Augustine does not think all these emotions — grief, in particular — will persist in the life of the resurrected in heaven. Nevertheless — and this is an enormous qualification that utterly transforms the ancient eudaimonistic ideal — what may have no place in the next life is not only appropriate but also necessary in this one. Here and now we are not at the end of our earthly pilgrimage. Here and now we suffer the loss of good things and people whom we quite rightly love. Here and now, therefore, we ought to experience grief, loss, and brokenness. If we did not, "while we are subject to the weakness of this life, there would really be something wrong with our life." Here and now, that is, we are not "happy." If the ideal of passionlessness is taken to mean a life in which no inappropriate emotions ("in defiance of reason") appear, "it is clearly a good and desirable state; but it does not belong to this present life" (14.9). To put it in the terms Augustine uses in the *Confessions* to describe the hurdle over which the Platonists had been unable to take him, one must learn the difference between presumption and confession (7.20). It would be presumption to imagine that we could attain the happiness we desire in this life. We may see the goal for which we yearn, but we must also confess that we cannot yet hold firmly to the way that leads there.

One might conclude, therefore, that grief is appropriate in this life because — but only because — we are not fully perfected. We remain sinners, inordinately attached to earthly goods, and what we grieve over is the sin that still clings to us. Nicholas Wolterstorff has developed such an argument, suggesting that Augustine does not approve of grief over the loss of earthly things, but only of grief over the fact that we are too attached to earthly goods and less than fully attached to God.[6] Over that sin we should grieve, but not over the loss of life's attachments and sweetness.

> The response Augustine urged to the grief which ensues upon change and decay in the objects we love is that we detach ourselves from such objects and attach ourselves to God in whom there is no shadow of turning. But this newly oriented self never wholly wins out over the old. And over that repetitious reappearance of the old self, the new now grieves. The *passive* grief of negated affection is replaced by the *active* grief of lamenting over the faults of one's religious character — over those persistent habits of the heart that one now recognizes as sin. (p. 201)

What Augustine (and "that long tradition of Christian piety which he helped to shape") gives us, Wolterstorff claims, is "a radical and comprehensive lowering of the worth of the things of this world" (p. 228). This leads in turn to an understanding of contentment as a virtue that trains us to ask little of the world — "to reconstruct one's self so as to be content under tyranny" rather than trying to overcome the tyrant (p. 229).

I offered some evidence above to suggest that this is an inadequate reading of Augustine.[7] For example, although it may

---

6. Nicholas Wolterstorff, "Suffering Love," in *Philosophy and the Christian Faith,* ed. Thomas V. Morris (Notre Dame, Ind.: University of Notre Dame Press, 1988), pp. 196-237. Parenthetical page references in the following text are to this work.

7. James Wetzel argues for a similar conclusion. Asking whether a perfect faith would rule out grief of the sort Augustine experienced at Monica's death, Wetzel writes: "On the contrary, it is what allows grief its truest expression: sorrow, pure and simple, over the loss of a beloved. We will miss the person who continues to be with God, but who is no longer with us." See

serve well as a reading of Augustine's account of the death of his friend in book 4 of the *Confessions*, I cannot see that it does justice to the pathos of his (decade-and-a-half-later) description of grief at the loss of friends in *City of God* 19.8. "As he gets older," James Wetzel writes, "Augustine gets less tempted to heap contempt directly upon the vulnerable beauties of this life, but he never quite gets over his desire for a world-disdaining faith."[8] Perhaps, then, we should move beyond asking only what position Augustine held. There were, after all, "two men" struggling within him, the struggle never came to an end, and surely there was something to be said for each of these men. If we join Augustine in his struggle, we face one of the most persistent problems for Christian life. How can we rightly grieve the loss of earthly attachments without idolatrously loving them as only God should be loved?

The problem of grief is shaped by the difficulty we have in thinking of created things always and only in relation to God. The good things of this world are real but not ultimate. Their independence is always a relative independence, since they can never exist entirely on their own, apart from the divine goodness that holds them and in which, simply by existing, they participate. It may be, therefore, that when we experience appropriate grief over loss, we often — always? — have a kind of dual experience: rightly sorrowing over the loss of some created good that gives life sweetness, and simultaneously wanting to have that good thing simply as our own (and not as God's gift). We may, that is, be hard pressed to say what a rightly ordered love for life's good things should look like. But

---

James Wetzel, "Book Four: The Trappings of Woe and Confession of Grief," in *A Reader's Companion to Augustine's "Confessions,"* p. 68.

8. Wetzel, p. 68.

that need not mean there is nothing to grieve except the continuing disorder of our love.

When in *City of God* Augustine describes this life as a school of virtue, he says we enjoy our earthly blessings "in the manner of pilgrims" (1.29). He says we are "not attached" to these blessings, and were that all he says, Wolterstorff's reading might be adequate. But it is not all Augustine says. Though not attached to earthly goods, we do "enjoy" them "in the manner of pilgrims." We care not only about the goal for which they school us but also about the blessings themselves. Sometimes it will hurt when we lose them, even though we may recognize that hurt as part of the schooling we need. As C. S. Lewis writes, "The settled happiness and security which we all desire, God withholds from us by the very nature of the world: but joy, pleasure, and merriment He has scattered broadcast. . . . Our Father refreshes us on the journey with some pleasant inns, but will not encourage us to mistake them for home."[9]

It is not easy to find language in which to express clearly the proper way to love something that is good, but good only relatively — something that has real but not ultimate value because it has no existence apart from its participation in the life that comes from God. Rather than saying it is not right to love earthly things, we should say we do not know the right way to love them. Hence, we should experience grief over both the loss of good things (which it is right to love) and the way in which we love them (which is often not right). If Augustine sometimes fails to get either his formulations or his loves in perfect order, we may not find it all that easy to do better (in either thought or in deed); for to think with Augustine about

9. C. S. Lewis, *The Problem of Pain* (New York: Macmillan, 1962), p. 115.

grief is to think about a problem that must be lived more than resolved.

Without supposing that he has resolved this problem for Christian life, Kierkegaard provides a formulation that draws us into the lived experience of grief and captures both its necessity and the constant danger that we may envision the things and persons we love as freestanding rather than as sharers in a life that comes from and is continually sustained by God. "But this 'You shall sorrow' is both true and beautiful. I do not have the right to harden myself against the pains of life, for I *ought* to sorrow; but neither have I the right to despair, for I *ought* to sorrow; furthermore, neither do I have the right to stop sorrowing, for I *ought* to sorrow."[10] Sorrow is appropriate, for as William Werpehowski comments, as creatures of God we are "bidden to enjoy the goods of creation."[11] Despair is inappropriate — for the good that has been lost, though real, is not ultimate.

We should not pretend that this is an easy word; indeed, it is hard in two quite different ways. The counsel that we ought to sorrow is hard, for it opens up before us the truth of Augustine's vision of life: namely, it hurts. Placed here among goods that rightly claim our love and attachment, we are also always on the way — and loss will be an inseparable part of this journey. Not to love the good things of this life, to practice Stoic detachment, might protect us against the pangs of grief, but it would mean that we had stepped off the path that leads to God. So we must continue that pilgrimage — and doing so will hurt.

10. Søren Kierkegaard, *Works of Love,* trans. Howard Hong and Edna Hong (New York: Harper Torchbooks, 1962), p. 57.

11. Werpehowski, p. 178.

The counsel that we ought not despair is, for different reasons, just as hard. Wolterstorff articulates why we might find it hard: "Nothing in this world has [for Augustine] worth enough to merit an attachment which carries the potential of grief — nothing except the religious state of souls. The state of my child's soul is worth suffering love; the child's company is not."[12] I have already made clear that I do not, in the end, think this is an accurate reading of Augustine, but it demonstrates how the lived experience of grief may often teeter uneasily between (permitted) sorrow and (forbidden) despair. It is right to love earthly things, but we do not know the right way to love them. We should suffer grief over their loss; we should suffer grief over our failure to love rightly. And somehow we must learn the humility that loves the goods of this life "in God," knowing that apart from that relation they cannot truly be themselves. Tempted to despair, we struggle to learn (only) to grieve. One cannot despair and simultaneously live in hope, but pilgrims on the way to God, gradually coming to be marked by the virtue of hope, ought to sorrow.

Paradoxical as it may seem, therefore, there is one sense in which we are in this life nearest to God when we are least like God. C. S. Lewis distinguished what he called "nearness-by-likeness" from "nearness-of-approach."[13] If there is fullness of joy in God's presence, that does not mean that experiencing grief draws us away from God; on the contrary, it may bring us nearer. "Let us suppose," Lewis writes, offering an analogy, "that we are doing a mountain walk to the village which is our home. At mid-day we come to the top of a cliff where we are, in

12. Wolterstorff, p. 228.

13. C. S. Lewis, *The Four Loves* (New York: Harcourt Brace Jovanovich, 1960), p. 15.

space, very near it because it is just below us. We could drop a stone into it. But as we are no cragsmen we can't get down. We must go a long way round; five miles, maybe. At many points during that *détour* we shall, statically, be farther from the village than we were when we sat above the cliff. But only statically. In terms of progress we shall be far 'nearer' our baths and teas."[14] To be on the way, therefore, even to suffer grief that is not transmuted into joy, grief we hope one day to leave behind when we are drawn more fully into God's life, is only to lack "nearness-by-likeness." But within the school of virtue that is human history, we may be approaching closer to the rest in God that is our desire.

We avoid presumption, therefore, when we hold firmly to the way that constitutes our approach to God — a way that can have no model other than the Word made flesh, of whom the Platonists had not been able to teach Augustine, the incarnate God whose story tells of "the face and look of pity, the tears of confession" (7.21). It is a story of grief, which, though transformed into joy within the divine life, can only be experienced as grief in "the Divine life operating under human conditions."[15]

To think of grief as constitutive of the believer's journey toward God places a premium on patience, the virtue that "accounts for the coincidence of joy and sorrow" along the pilgrim's way.[16] This patience, at least as a Christian virtue, is not simply an acceptance of necessity; it is "obedience to holy personal will."[17] Perhaps even — though we enter here into mys-

14. Lewis, *The Four Loves*, pp. 15-16.
15. Lewis, *The Four Loves*, p. 17.
16. Werpehowski, p. 178.
17. David Baily Harned, *Patience: How We Wait upon the World* (Boston: Cowley Publications, 1997), p. 84.

teries well beyond my ability to unpack — there is a sense in which suffering and patience do have a place in heaven, even if they are there always and immediately transmuted into joy. Even in the life of the triune God, a life of perfect mutual love, we might say that a certain minimal self-adherence must be constantly overcome. "The doctrine of the Trinity affirms that the status of patient is essential to the perfection of divine activity. . . . All of those who have found a social analogy useful for approaching the mystery of the divine life . . . have recognized that the suffering which companionship involves is at the heart of divine omnipotence."[18] From eternity the Father gives his life to the Son, who offers that begotten life back to the Father in perfect obedience, through the bond of love that is the Spirit. We must try to picture the three persons "each defining its own identity in genuine otherness, each losing itself in common enterprise pursued without jealousy or conflict, so at one that each was in the all."[19] Patience not only marks the pilgrim's way, therefore; it also, mysteriously, characterizes the goal of that way.

For now, however, if our desire for God is serious, it is "nearness-of-approach" that must be the focus of our attention. As Augustine puts it in the *Confessions*, "he who cannot see you for the distance, may yet walk along the road by which he will arrive and see you and lay hold on you" (7.21). This way of approach will sometimes bring great joy, but also great sor-

18. Harned, p. 180. Although Augustine is not usually named as an architect of a "social analogy" for the Trinity, one can find adumbrations of it in his thought. See his *The Trinity*, trans. Edmund Hill, O.P., in *The Works of Saint Augustine: A Translation for the 21st Century* (Brooklyn: New City Press, 1991), 8.5.14: "Now love means someone loving and something loved with love. There you are with three, the lover, what is being loved, and love."

19. William C. Placher, *Narratives of a Vulnerable God* (Louisville: Westminster John Knox, 1994), p. 71.

row, as it sets before us others whom it is our duty to love here and now — so that then and there they may share with us "the land of peace in the distance."

METHOD

I HAVE LEFT till last a brief word about method, about what I take myself to have been doing in the previous chapters — attempting, as I have sometimes put it, to think with Augustine about important aspects of the moral life. I do not by any means think a discussion of method ought to be our primary focus. I have not forgotten how struck I was, when I began graduate study at Princeton more than thirty years ago, by the tendency of conversations in the lounge of 1879 Hall to focus on questions of method in the study of religion. Often these conversations were quite interesting, but only gradually did I come to realize that the focus of our discussions was so single-mindedly on method because we had few substantive beliefs in common. Method alone was our shared possession, what we could talk about. It is worth a word here.

I cannot say, however, that I first developed a method and then used it in the reading of Augustine. The methodological reflections here are much more after the fact, an attempt to think about what I have been doing. One might say, after all, that I have been thinking with Augustine less for the sake of being able to elucidate what he says than for the sake of entering, with and through him, into a centuries-long conversation about the shape of the Christian life.

In those puzzling last books of the *Confessions,* when his attention turns to interpreting the opening verses of Genesis, Augustine himself is forced to consider a certain question of method. He offers a reading of what Moses says in Genesis, realizing that another interpreter, without denying the truth of what Augustine says, may offer a different reading of what Moses had in mind. With that in itself Augustine has no problem. There may be an "abundance of perfectly true meanings which can be extracted" from the text of Genesis (12.25). Rather than asserting that one and only one of these true meanings was what Moses had in mind, Augustine is quite prepared to learn from any of them that have discerned some truth. "I hope, therefore," he writes, in a passage it is hard not to enjoy, "to avoid being pestered by the kind of person who says: 'Moses did not think as you say; he thought as I say'" (12.25). We should, Augustine thinks, love our own opinion about the matters the text treats not because it is our own, but because it is true. And if we love it for that reason, we should love any other true opinion for the very same reason — a lesson that, if taken to heart, will make us less possessive about our views. Thus Augustine says of the position of those who disagree with him about Genesis: "In fact it [their interpretation of Moses] ceases to be theirs just because it is true. If, therefore, they love it because it is true, then it is both theirs and mine; it is the common property of all lovers of truth" (12.25).

To some degree, therefore, I have been reading Augustine as if he were our contemporary, trying to think with him in order to get some insight into the truth of how we ought to live. Clearly, this is not the way an historian would approach him, carefully locating him within his own time and place. To read him as I have done risks, therefore, ignoring the actual circumstances in which he lived and underplaying or ignoring things that were important to him. Nor would I claim — as too easy a way out here — that "any appropriation of a historical figure is always, if only implicitly, for the sake of present circumstances."[1] I doubt whether that claim is true, and, in any case, I cannot imagine how I would prove it. So it is necessary that we have more strictly circumscribed historical work, which eschews any direct attempt at informing or shaping our own moral self-understanding. Indeed, if we too single-mindedly attempt to instruct or form the views of our contemporaries, our work may become more narrow or shallow than it need be. Thus, the work of historians is essential, and I have tried at various points to profit from it.

It is worth noting in passing, however, that those who style themselves historians do not always write about figures such as Augustine as if their chief concern were simply to help the rest of us understand him in his time and place. Thus, for example, in his recent biography of Augustine, James O'Donnell aims to make Augustine's Christianity "unfamiliar to us," to "imagine Augustine without the future we know he had," to help us see "for the first time what we might think is already well known" — in short, to distance Augustine from us.[2] Yet, when O'Donnell proposes very early in his narrative to take a few pages "to set out in the simplest terms" and "without comment" the story Augustine himself told in the *Confessions*, he can scarcely complete a paragraph without offering his own

1. Michael Hanby, *Augustine and Modernity* (London and New York: Routledge, 2003), pp. 3-4.

2. James J. O'Donnell, *Augustine: A New Biography* (New York: Harper-Collins, 2005). Cf. pp. 181, 189, and 217-18.

comment. The story of the theft of pears is "recounted at puzzling length," and we have good reason to suspect that Augustine "rather overdid the accusations against his younger self." His study of philosophy led to "religious zealotry," one form of which, Manicheism, "had a bad rap with right-thinking people in the fourth century and hasn't recovered much since." And so it goes throughout a biography that, under the guise of history, renders philosophical judgments about whether notions such as "soul" can still make sense, offers theological speculation about the possibility of a catholicism that might include "more religious traditions than the ones that can claim a home in Jerusalem," repeatedly asserts without argument that Saint Paul was the true founder of Christianity, regards as foolish Augustine's notion (not all that different from a recent claim of "postliberalism") that the biblical books might define the world, characterizes (though without any serious attempt to analyze) as "unintentionally comical" Augustine's attempt to imagine what unfallen sexuality would be like, and engages in countless "what if" speculations about what Augustine's life or our world might have been like had various events not occurred. This is by no means strictly circumscribed historical study, and it is less likely to achieve distance than to intrude unanalyzed contemporary prejudices. Perhaps, therefore, others who want to try to think with Augustine may be forgiven if they make no claims to be historians.

Yet, even where the work of historians is far more circumspect and helpful, theirs is not the only way to read or the only reason for reading a thinker such as Augustine. An example may help. In his classic biography of Augustine, Peter Brown — an historian from whom a great deal can certainly be learned — writing about Augustine's views on sexuality and noting that, in his time and place, those views were in certain respects quite moderate, says: "We must never read Augustine as if he were contemporary with ourselves."³ We understand what Brown means. He is concerned that we may do Augustine an injustice — seeing his views about sex as much odder than they were in his day — if we rip them from their historical context. Salutary as that warning is, however, there is also another danger: we may make a thinker as significant as Augustine seem largely irrelevant to our concerns and questions, even when those concerns touch the deepest recesses of human life. By contrast, Richard Rorty notes that

analytic philosophers who have attempted "rational reconstructions" of the arguments of great dead philosophers have done so in the hope of treating these philosophers as contemporaries, as colleagues with whom they can exchange views. . . . Such reconstructions, however, have led to charges of anachronism. . . . There seems to be a dilemma: either we anachronistically impose enough of our problems and vocabulary on the dead to make them conversational partners, or we confine our interpretive activity to making their falsehoods look less silly by placing them in the context of the benighted times in which they were written.⁴

3. Peter Brown, *Augustine of Hippo: A Biography*, a new edition with an epilogue (Berkeley and Los Angeles: University of California Press, 2000), p. 500.

4. Richard Rorty, "The Historiography of Philosophy: Four Genres," in *Philosophy in History: Essays on the Historiography of Philosophy*, ed. Richard Rorty, J. B. Schneewind, and Quentin Skinner (Cambridge: University Press, 1984), p. 49. For a more poignant expression of such a possibility, consider Machiavelli's words in one of his letters to Francesco Vettori: "When evening comes, I go back home, and go to my study. On the threshold I take off my work clothes, covered in mud and filth, and put on the clothes an ambassador

If we pass by the chronological snobbery that inclines Rorty to see previous ages as inevitably benighted, we can discern here a sense of why it might be important also to read Augustine as our contemporary and conversation partner, with whom we can think and from whom we may learn.[5]

This way of reading may depend in considerable measure on a belief — central, I think, to humanistic studies — that many questions are never really "answered" in a way that makes continued reflection on them unprofitable or pointless. Thus, for example, I am baffled when I find an excellent scholar writing that "the substantive issues that Anders Nygren attempted to raise in his discussion of Augustine in these categories [i.e., agape and eros] were answered as long ago as J. Burnaby's now classic *Amor Dei*."[6] That Burnaby provides a serious and in many respects persuasive response to Nygren, who can doubt? But an "answer" that closes off the fruitfulness of continued conversation about a book as great as Nygren's? This is to picture humanistic learning as far too much like a modern science — vertically structured in a way that makes present expertise depend rather little on study of previous generations.

---

would wear. Decently dressed, I enter the ancient courts of rulers who have long since died. There I am warmly welcomed, and I feed on the only food I find nourishing, and was born to savor. I am not ashamed to talk to them, and to ask them to explain their actions. And they, out of kindness, answer me." This letter (of December 10, 1513) is translated in Niccolò Machiavelli, *The Prince*, ed. and trans. David Wootton (Indianapolis and Cambridge: Hackett, 1995). For this passage see p. 3.

5. Thus Rorty adds, correctly I think: "Those alternatives, however, do not constitute a dilemma. We should do both of these things, but do them separately" (Rorty, p. 49).

6. Lewis Ayres, "Augustine, Christology, and God as Love: An Introduction to the Homilies on I John," in *Nothing Greater, Nothing Better: Theological Essays on the Love of God*, ed. Kevin J. Vanhoozer (Grand Rapids: Eerdmans, 2001), p. 92 n. 40.

In fact, however, much of what we learn about human nature and human life comes from gradually working our way into a tradition of thought and learning from predecessors within it, especially those who are acknowledged masters. In many other areas of human endeavor — hitting a baseball, playing jazz, diagnosing a patient — we obviously learn by imitating others whose excellence we can see. We are not always as ready to grant that this is also true of, say, learning to think as a Christian about the moral life. Yet, thinking with someone like Augustine is often the way to gain genuine insight, which is something very different from simple repetition. And it turns out quite often that we are still engaged with issues Augustine wrote about — not surprisingly, since his reach extends far enough to shape the discussions in which we find ourselves. This does not mean that we simply accept what he says; after all, we think with him just as much when we are moved to (at least partial) disagreement or to puzzlement.

In his introduction to the first volume of *The Jewish Political Tradition*, Michael Walzer describes that volume's attempt to draw together different Jewish texts on political topics and offer, in addition, contemporary commentary on them. "Although," he writes, "a scheme of this kind can be, and should be, historically sensitive, its primary aim is not historical verisimilitude."[7] The writers whose texts are gathered together in the volume

> live in a particular time and place; they are faithful to local customs and practices; and they are often deeply involved

7. Michael Walzer, "Introduction: The Jewish Political Tradition," in *The Jewish Political Tradition*, vol. 1, *Authority*, ed. Michael Walzer, Menachem Lorberbaum, and Noam J. Zohar (New Haven and London: Yale University Press, 2000), p. xxvii.

in local political struggles and intellectual debates. We [the editors and commentators] can only rarely capture these local engagements in a work of this sort. They are the province of the historian, and readers interested in them should consult one of the standard histories. We highlight only the larger, recurrent issues, the long-term responses (or the ongoing arguments about how to respond) to reiterated political and intellectual challenges. This is the province of the political theorist, who can also ask what characteristic form these issues and responses take and what we have to learn from them. How should we engage with and carry on this tradition of thought? What in it needs to be criticized, or revised, or abandoned?[8]

This manner of thinking, more philosophical than historical, is one way we learn from the past. In a short essay published elsewhere Walzer illustrates — from the discipline of political theory — why each way has its place.

In the 1950s there was an extraordinary outpouring of books and articles about Thomas Hobbes. Scholars, mostly philosophers, read *Leviathan,* Hobbes's major treatise, published in 1651, as if it had just appeared — thus correcting for the accident of death. Imagine, they seemed to be saying, that this man Hobbes has recently been given tenure at Harvard. Is that a mistake? How good are the arguments in *Leviathan?* . . .

Responding critically to the writers of the 50s and elaborating their own views in the following decades, another group of scholars, mostly historians, argued for a very dif-

8. Walzer, "Introduction," p. xxvii.

ferent process of recovery. They insisted that the only way to understand Hobbes, or any writer in the canon, is to read him from within his time and place. The text must be put in its historical context, because its most authoritative readers were its first readers, for whom it was originally written, who knew its circumstances and presuppositions, and who grasped its idioms without editorial help.[9]

Without in any way dismissing the worth of the second approach, granting in fact its considerable achievements in helping us to understand better what Hobbes was doing when he wrote, Walzer also notes that an exclusive diet of that approach can cost us something. "It is less clear why such books should matter to us."[10] For it is the more philosophical approach — reading with Hobbes or Augustine about questions that engaged them and engage us still, treating them as ongoing partners in the conversation about such questions — that keeps alive for us the truth that there are recurring questions (and answers), not just countless different, individual (situated and contextualized) questions and answers.

Only thus can we have a genuine tradition of thought that, without trapping us in the past or simply reiterating it, takes our shared humanity seriously enough to believe that we remain connected to those earlier thinkers and the generations of people for whom they wrote. As Servais Pinckaers says of Aquinas, "Can one not say that through his dialogue with Aristotle, Thomas has become a contemporary of the Philosopher, or, if you will, that he has introduced him into his own age,

---

9. Michael Walzer, "Philosophy, History, and the Recovery of Tradition," *Chronicle of Higher Education*, June 16, 2000, p. A56.

10. Walzer, "Philosophy," p. A56.

and into the University of Paris, as a contemporary master? Can one not likewise think that Aristotle and Thomas may become our contemporaries, masters present to the modern reader as well . . . ? This is, perhaps, still clearer in the case of Augustine, who has been called the most modern of the fathers of the church."[11] If this is a method, we might call it an "ecumenism of time," for which the dead are never simply left behind. This seems especially appropriate for Christian theological reflection, since, after all, in the Eucharist we share the praise of God with "all the company of saints" — among them, I trust, Augustine of Hippo. If that can possibly be true — and the church affirms it weekly — I see no reason why we may not try to think with Augustine as I have done here.

---

11. Servais-Théodore Pinckaers, O.P., "The Sources of the Ethics of St. Thomas Aquinas," in *The Ethics of Aquinas*, ed. Stephen J. Pope (Washington, D.C.: Georgetown University Press, 2002), p. 27.

INDEX